Young Writers

POETRY COMPETITION

GREAT MINDS

Your World...Your Future...YOUR WORDS

From South East England
Edited by Steve Twelvetree

 Young**Writers**

First published in Great Britain in 2005 by:
Young Writers
Remus House
Coltsfoot Drive
Peterborough
PE2 9JX
Telephone: 01733 890066
Website: www.youngwriters.co.uk

SB ISBN 1 84460 889 1

Foreword

This year, the Young Writers' 'Great Minds' competition proudly presents a showcase of the best poetic talent selected from over 40,000 up-and-coming writers nationwide.

Young Writers was established in 1991 to promote the reading and writing of poetry within schools and to the youth of today. Our books nurture and inspire confidence in the ability of young writers and provide a snapshot of poems written in schools and at home by budding poets of the future.

The thought, effort, imagination and hard work put into each poem impressed us all and the task of selecting poems was a difficult but nevertheless enjoyable experience.

We hope you are as pleased as we are with the final selection and that you and your family continue to be entertained with *Great Minds From South East England* for many years to come.

Contents

Dormers Wells High School, Southall

Enfield County School, Enfield

Furness Special School, Swanley

Northwood College, Northwood

Sumayya Merali (12)	78
Stephanie Bryan-Kinns (12)	79
Charleen Sylvian-Shantaruban (12)	80
Georgina Dunlop (12)	80
Nikita Shah (12)	81
Helena Lewczynska (12)	81
Monal Shah (12)	82
Jessica Lancod-Frost (12)	82
Charlotte Rome (12)	83
Reena Shah (13)	83
Meera Bhudia (13)	84
Meera Shah (12)	84
Ishleen Kaur (12)	85
Dipali Amin (12)	86
Reshma Dhamecha (12)	87
Priya Uka (12)	88
Caroline Perkins (13)	88
Laura Smith (12)	89
Aarthi Jegatheeswaran (12)	89
Sara Asaria (12)	90
Yasmin Patel (12)	90
Emma Teboul (14)	91
Alexa Fitzpatrick (12)	91
Rosie Griggs (13)	92
Rebecca Bingham (12)	92
Alexandra Kleist-Patchett (13)	93
Alice Blakeley (14)	93
Priyanka Kotecha (13)	94
Falguni Karia (13)	94
Rachna Patel (13)	95
Zainab Mustafa (13)	95
Sruti Dupaguntla (12)	96
Lilian Knight (13)	96
Sophie Wright (13)	97
Zara Malik (13)	97
Anika Parmar (12)	98
Jessie Stern (13)	99
Charlotte West (12)	99
Sonali Shah (12)	100
Sarah Sayeed (12)	100
Roshni Kanabar (13)	101

The Matthew Arnold School, Staines

The Poems

Mirror Reflection . . .

(Dedicated to all my good friends)

Your love was one I tried to fulfil,
That was my one and only will.

Our love is now forever bound,
Deep inside where it won't be found.

My love was one ready to grow,
But this time you dipped really low.

The things you did and said,
It didn't have to turn out that way.

Our love was supposed to be a happy ending,
Why are you still pretending?

Every time I ask you, you lie
Please answer me why?

In love I have lost all hope,
But love will also find a way to cope.

Kanda Ahmed (14)

Brightly

Brightly the colours swift into autumn leaves,
Brightly the glowing sun weaves.
Brightly the stars glimmer into their place,
Brightly the moon stares up into space.

Brightly the city lights are lit,
Brightly the child's night light fits.
Bright as the television - but the chandelier is more,
The cat's eyes shimmer, beside the cabinet door.

Saira Hussein (12)

Shallow Society

People look at me
But don't go deeper than the skin
They judge me by appearance
Not by what's within.

My interior is very weak
Although I may look strong
I'm not, I'm easily broken
But the bullying carries on.

Because I'm not size 10
With the bra size of D
Doesn't mean you can carry on
Endlessly torturing me.

OK, so I'm not thin
But you don't have the right,
To bully me all day
And then again at night.

Stupid boarding school
I can never get away,
Don't judge me by my size
Or, how much I weigh.

People wonder then
Why I want to end my life
But they just send me to shrinks
And take away my knives.

Perhaps if someone helped me
I might just change my mind
But first go deeper than my skin
And see what you might find.

Jenny Halliday (15)

My Dearest Friend (RIP)

My friend was really crazy,
My friend was really nuts,
She tried to ban smoking
But burned down the school huts!

My friend drove me bananas,
My friend was very batty,
She tried to paint her mum's new car
Which made her mum quite ratty.

My friend was rather foolish,
My friend was absolutely mad,
She ate some mouldy bread (for a dare)
Which made her tummy feel bad.

My friend was extremely happy,
My friend was so much fun.
She lived life on the edge
And always carried a toy gun.

My friend did lots of weird things,
There's not enough room to scribble them all down,
But I will have all the memories
Of my dearest friend who was the class clown.

My friend wanted to be a comedian.
She loved to have a joke
And she liked to entertain
With every word she spoke.

Now that friend has gone,
My world has been torn apart.
She was taken by leukaemia,
But she will always be in my heart.

Shaunna Jane Butler (13)
Bentley Wood High School, Stanmore

Our Birdy, RIP

Birdy Purdy sat on the wall,
Birdy Purdy had a great fall.
All of his bird friends and all of his chicks,
Couldn't put him together because he landed on bricks.

Birdy Purdy went to the medical centre,
He thought he'd be fine before he did enter.
The doctor checked his cracked open head,
And then put him safe and soundly to bed.

Birdy Purdy is now really upset,
No longer a bird but now a pet.
Not only a Chihuahua but other things too,
A chameleon, parakeet and one eye of green goo.

Three days later he died a tragic death,
He escaped from his house and waved to Beth.
The child was in shock when she saw him leave,
He gave her a dirty look, which made her peeved.

Birdy got run over by a car,
His guts flew over to Dar Es Salaam.
Oh Birdy why did you leave?
You left us all alone to grieve.

Now you're six foot underground,
Not making your cheerful, bubbly sound.
Oh Birdy we'll never forget you,
You were a living dream come true.

Suhaylah Chatoo & Sabiha Kaba (13)
Bentley Wood High School, Stanmore

Death

Death will come and take me one day
But when that day comes; I will never know
Because I and everyone has a time to die
And it won't matter if we have riches and plenty of dough.

Death is one great wonder
When our time will end
When we can't repair
And leaves us to deeply ponder.

One day you might not wake alive
To continue what you started
Or finish what you've dreamt
Just try and take it like a permanent dive.

We also won't know what will happen after we die
Obviously no one has lived to tell the tale
But all we know is to be good
And not say at all one lie.

Apparently we leave our body here
So our soul will go to a 'better place'
Our then deserted body will be buried or cremated
Our feelings until then might be full of fear.

What will happen when we die?
This is always the question
But then again there is always a mixed reaction
We know just that after many people feel to cry.

Annum Qureshi (13)
Bentley Wood High School, Stanmore

Parents?

Parents?
What are they?
Who are they?
What are they like?
I'll tell you, and maybe you'll agree.

They're aliens from space,
Who landed on Earth with a mace.

They can be fussy,
And are always bossy.

Their nose goes rosy
When they become really nosy.

They have a weird mind,
So they're usually kind.

They can drive you mad,
And punish you if you're bad.

They make you eat cabbage,
And all the other garbage.

They have a good sense of humour,
However, they'll believe any rumour.

They never call you names,
But are forever after fame.

They can be a pest,
But to be honest, they are the best!

Suhaila Mohamed (13)
Bentley Wood High School, Stanmore

Ghost

He was walking down an alley,
Until he saw someone strange
There he was, all alone,
The atmosphere changed.

He tried to walk faster,
But his feet slowed down.
There was a grip, a clutch,
He made no sound.

There was a painful cry
As the blade went through,
A young boy on the ground,
His death was due.

Fifty spears in a body,
Arrows too,
The scream of a child,
That's all he knew.

He felt himself rise,
As he got up from the ground,
But then to his horror,
His spirit was unbound.

He saw himself lying,
Lying there dead.
But how could this be?
As he was hovering overhead.

Yes, it's true
I know what you're thinking,
You must be stone-cold,
Not even blinking.

This was a long time ago
Near the edgy coast
Brace yourself, get ready
He'd become a ghost!

Vrinda Sodha (14)
Bentley Wood High School, Stanmore

Mother

I sit in the park where I dwell
For mother's love so well . . .

Her loving nature has flourished within my soul
My mother completes me, she makes me whole . . .

She's the one I shared my dreams with . . .
The one who taught me in more ways than one

My mother is God's gift to me
She's an angel sent from Heaven

When I look at her I see
All those years she's devoted to me

And now that she's gone . . .
I realise everything I took for granted

Those days we spent apart
Feel like an eternity

I long for the reassurance in her voice
When I've done something wrong

The comfort and warmth in her arms
Is where I belong

I love her with all my heart
I have done right from the start

But does she know how I feel?
Pain; which only she can heal . . .

Without her, I cannot imagine life
So where is she now that I need her by my side?

She's in my mind all the time
In my answers, my questions
My dreams, and everywhere around me

She's the secret I cannot hide
The past which I cannot forget . . .

But a voice in my heart tells me
The distance has now parted

Where is she . . . ?
She's in my heart . . .

Samina Sulaman (14)
Bentley Wood High School, Stanmore

The Cruelty Of Man

I am all alone now,
They killed my parents,
My brothers, my sisters.
There is no one left but me.
Do they even care what they are doing to us?
Where are we to live?
Would they like it if we did it to them?
No, I'm sure they wouldn't.

Cutting down grand trees,
Just so they can live a life of luxury.
Do they even wait to think
Of just how many animals they are killing
Just so they can earn a living?

Whilst their lives are booming,
Ours are slowly fading away.
When we are gone forever,
People will realise what they did was wrong
But it'll be too late then.
You've done your destruction;
Now there's no turning back.

Ria Pattni (13)
Bentley Wood High School, Stanmore

School's Out!

School's out,
For one whole week,
So I can lie in bed,
And get more sleep.

I wake up happy,
Remembering that it's half-term,
I don't have to study,
Because there's no one to learn or teach.

Half-term is the time,
To play and mess about,
But when you're back at school,
You're not allowed to shout.

As half-term ends,
I'm excited to go back to school,
As it is the time to learn,
But don't forget your writing tools.

Priyanka Patel (13)
Bentley Wood High School, Stanmore

Homelessness

H ostels are my home from time to time,
O utstayed my welcome,
M y life was once a dream but it seems as if it never happened,
E ating out of dustbins, searching for food,
L ying in doorways is not the life I dreamt of,
E ach night I go to sleep and I wonder if I will wake up,
S craps for dinner, breakfast and lunch,
S leeping roughly,
N obody to care for me or tuck me into bed,
E nemies are lurking about,
S leeping in all weather conditions,
S tepping into the big wide world is harder than I thought.

Gemma Ward (13)
Bentley Wood High School, Stanmore

Time

Time . . . the most valuable asset
Sometimes it flies away so swiftly
That you don't realise
Then it never comes back to you.

Time means limit
A limit for everything,
For happiness and joy,
And for unhappiness and sorrow.

Time doesn't wait for anyone or anything
Without time, there would be no challenges in life
Time is so precious,
Time is so valuable.

Time is maths
Time is music
Time is science
Time is everything.

Cheta Patel (13)
Bentley Wood High School, Stanmore

Hallowe'en

H air-raising spooky tales of witches and ghouls
A nd children trick or treating as broomsticks fill the air.
L oud, cackling laughter as the witches scare the fools
L earning new spells as the cauldron boils a brew that's rare.
O utside all the black cats gather, miaowing their hellos;
W ondering which broomstick they will ride tonight.
E very vampire is out after dark . . . such ugly fellows!
E vening is the time for werewolves . . . they love to bite!
N early over for another year, *thank goodness!*

Charlotte Radette (13)
Bentley Wood High School, Stanmore

Love

My need to be held in the cold cruel nights,
Grows and grows as the cold wind bites.
The fulfilling feeling I'd get from your touch,
Reminds me of your warm face so much.
The visions I get of you in my dreams
Are not as real as they seem.
Life moves so fast and won't slow down,
I stop and remember when you were around.
You'd hold me tight and wipe all my tears,
Said you'd be around for years and years.
Now you're gone, I'm on my own,
I tried to call but couldn't pick up the phone.
You'd found a place in my heart, mind and soul,
Words are stuck in my throat like a lump of coal.
I want to tell you how I feel,
It's because of you that my love is so real.
I don't understand why you wanted to go,
I need you more than you'll ever know.

Chandni Rawal (14)
Bentley Wood High School, Stanmore

The Feelings Within

Every time I'd see you my heart filled with joy,
I'd see your sweet smile and I'd drop to the floor
I'd look at your face and all I would see,
Are your beautiful brown eyes reflecting on me.

I'd hear just one second of your innocent voice,
And I'd feel my heart racing, thumping louder as it goes
Love is the feeling that no one can hide,
Love is the feeling you should abide.

Jamila Ahmed (13)
Bentley Wood High School, Stanmore

Darkness Is Mine

I wear loneliness
I hear the voices of dry leaves
The leaves of endless sadness
My painful eyes are sleepless
My lips are moving, but I am quiet
My face is full of scratches
Sun sets in my eyes, thus they are bright.

I am stone of the path
No one cares of my scream or yell
My useless existence hurts
My breaths are burden for me as well
I feel tears boil in my eyes
And I can feel them cry
My shaking lips are wet
My eyes are still dry.

The pain I feel in myself
Is really hard to heal,
My wounds are my wealth
I still want them to conceal.

My heart beats, or eyes blink, it stings
I don't want to fly from pain
Take away my wings
I am a dry-nature creation
It burns me when it rains
Whenever I think of you
I feel you, it pains
I live in darkness
I breathe at night, it's fine
I fear the sunshine
O light, don't sit next to me
Go . . . !
'Darkness is mine.'

Tahira Batool (13)
Bentley Wood High School, Stanmore

Owls

Their movements are soundless.
Their coats are quite sleek.
Their actions are harmless.
They screech when they speak.

Their language is wordless.
Their song is breathtaking.
Their wisdom is endless.
They send creatures shaking.

Their wingspan is vast.
Their nests are quite spacious.
Their prey has soon past.
Their gliding is gracious.

Their eyes are black saucers.
Their instinct is chasing.
Their soar is quite forceless.
Yet they are amazing.

Layla Hantouli (13)
Bentley Wood High School, Stanmore

Hero

A hero is self-confident, admirable and cool,
A person who is very wise and does not act like a fool.

A hero doesn't go to parties and drink himself all crazy,
But does something that is worthwhile, and is never lazy.

A hero doesn't need superpower,
To beat an amazing power.

A hero is well respected and unique in every way,
And if you really try, I think, you might be one someday.

Collin Abastillas (12)
Bentley Wood High School, Stanmore

Graffiti

Over the tracks
Back of the flats
It's growing
Like a garden.

Round the streets
All concrete
No grass, no trees
Nothing green.

But
Over the tracks
Back of the flats
It's growing
Like a garden.

There's every colour
You can think of
Every shape
Every size.

Words spark
Like fireworks
Jazzy, dazzling
Mind your eyes.

Zigzag letters
Fizzle and fall
Squiggles and splodges
Surprising the wall.

Tina Marunza (12)
Bentley Wood High School, Stanmore

Two Goth Angels

The poor Goth angel,
Sat in her cloud of salty tears,
As people laughed at her tattered wings.
She shivered as she thought of her fears.

She pitied every blade of grass
That was stamped on every day
Her heart turned black with her past,
Her life was just so grey.

Then one day, out of the blue
She bumped into a boy,
He was a Goth with tattered wings too
He called himself the wonderful Troy.

Their past was the same
They wanted a future together,
And they realised fate was to blame
So now they are together forever!

Helena Haciepiri (12)
Bentley Wood High School, Stanmore

Anger

A feeling of hate
A feeling of annoyance
A feeling of irritation
A bad feeling?
No!
The consequences are bad
People affected
Things broken
Things done that will be regretted
But anger itself?
Just another feeling that everybody feels.

Damilola Bajomo (14)
Bexley Grammar School, Welling

A Day In The Life Of A Fox

A ragged fox out on the prowl,
Not hearing the pack beginning to howl.

Just looking for some food to eat,
A chicken, rabbit, a tasty treat.

Wandering through the woods at night
Amongst the trees in the glowing moonlight.

A lone rabbit scuttles out of the ground,
The fox looks hungrily at what he has found.

A rustle in the bush, the rabbit's ears prick,
As the sly fox treads on a crackling stick.

A sudden gunshot pierces the night
The rabbit's gone in haste and fright.

The fox now frozen still with fear,
Sniffs the air and pricks his ears.

Four little cubs close by,
Oblivious to the hue and cry.

The pack draws nearer the scent is strong,
The hounds are eager, the chase is on.

Through the woods the fox does run
Away from hounds and hunter's gun.

The fox is quick and knows the way
He'll live to see another day.

Sophie McGery (13)
Bexley Grammar School, Welling

Wacky Family Races

'The family wacky races are speeding into town!
There's an assortment of cars from all around!
They're painted multicoloured, spotted and striped,
Bottle-green, sea-blue, red like an apple just ripened!
With bells, horns, engines and more!
For any citizen rich or poor!'
The commentators prattle on,
Whilst the automobiles have already gone!
Down the racetrack and over the hills,
Past the farms and numerous windmills!
'Let's tell you more about our drivers!
Our terrible losers and winning thrivers!
Look! There's Mr and Mrs Erdburly
They're a couple that share their lives compassionately!
Though unfortunately they are bemused very easily!
Watch out family Magbury!
And although their appearance is quite straggly,
This family of three, acts with utmost humility -
Whenever they win a race!
And in the lead are a mother and daughter,
Who apparently are rumoured never to falter!
They are quite an ambitious and competitive pair,
But they're always jolly and free of care!
And second to them is Mr Wilmy,
Representing his large Greek family,
He has a wide, expressionless face,
He's obviously concentrating hard on the race!
Suddenly his car jerks, he accelerates forwards,
He sees the finish line and continues onwards!
Past the mother and daughter now,
He smiles and wipes the soot off his brow!
He wins! His endeavour not in vain!
He drives proudly away from the racing lane!'
The losers are only slightly subdued,
They're not jealous, angry or rude,
But overjoyed that they took part,
And raced around in their racing cart,

They say many thanks and congratulations,
Enough racing! Now celebrations!
It was great fun! They partied 'til noon!
You better watch out, family wacky racing is coming your way soon!

Melissa Hicks (12)
Bexley Grammar School, Welling

Footballers

As they walk out onto the pitch,
I'm wondering why they're so rich.

Now here comes William Gelbert the referee
He's very strict, you wait and see.

The whistle's blown, only 5 minutes and already there's a penalty,
Here he comes, he strikes it right
The keeper dives and punches it with all his might.

Corner!

The ball comes in, but it's out by Jak
Now they can start a counter attack.

Finally here comes a good chance,
Moors with his stepover dance.

He goes left, he goes right,
Then he strikes it with all his might.

Goal!

Aaron Owusu (14)
Bexley Grammar School, Welling

Fear

A fear of spiders
A fear of heights,
A fear of snakes,
A fear of fright.

A fear of anger,
A fear of rats,
A fear of time,
A fear of cats.

A fear of trains,
A fear of sleep,
A fear of dogs,
A fear of dreams.

A fear of illness,
A fear of cars,
A fear of hospital,
A fear of scars.

A fear of secrets,
A fear of lying,
A fear of truth,
A fear of flying.

A new fear,
An old one,
A secret,
A told one.

My fear is different,
My fear is frank,
My fear is of
The page being blank.

Hannah Brennan (11)
Bexley Grammar School, Welling

My Party

In my party all has come
Apart from some
In my party all are wealthy
And all of them are healthy.

In my party the food is great
Everyone likes the chocolate cake
In my party the fish is nice
And so is the rice.

In my party all have come in style
Apart from some who are in denial
In my party all have come by steed
To join us and feed.

In my party all has been magnificent
But for us it wasn't insufficient
In my party the chandelier is made out of jade,
The party was so good everyone stayed.

Timothy Man (11)
Bexley Grammar School, Welling

The Spirit Of The Horse

I see him out of my window grazing gracefully
I see him rolling radically
I see him happily
I see him canter the field as friendly as can be
I see him neighing naughtily
I see him as angry as can be
I see him as a friend
I see him as a host
I see him as a horse.

Louise Dray (12)
Chapter School, Rochester

Snow!

Suddenly the sky turns grey,
And the snow falls on its way,
It's crystal and ice,
And looks very nice,
On that snowy day.

Suddenly the floor's all white,
Oh what a beautiful sight,
It's white and cold,
And easy to hold
On that snowy day.

Suddenly the sun shines down,
The white and snow is now gone,
It's back just right,
To the old normal sight,
On that snowy day.

Louise Eagle (12)
Chapter School, Rochester

Hallowe'en

Hallowe'en is scary,
It gives you a fright.
It makes you feel all shivery,
In the middle of the night.

Everyone in costumes,
Knocking on your doors
Trick or treat,
Can I have a sweet?

All the scary noises,
Can't get to sleep
What's that noise?
I hope it's not the ghoul!

Aimee Slater (13)
Chapter School, Rochester

My Bubble

You watch it rise;
You watch it float;
You watch as it tries;
To sink like a boat!

But it's no good,
It's gone too far,
Racing just like a car!

It's round and shiny
Sometimes it's tiny!
Although when it's slow,
It can shine like a rainbow.

And now it's high
High in the sky,
You watched it rise,
You watched it float;
You watched as it tries;
And now it cries!

Kirsty Mayle (12)
Chapter School, Rochester

All Alone

All alone on my own another day has gone
All alone on my own I eat a meal for one
All alone on my own sit down and fall asleep
A different day has come I make a meal for two
A different day has come there are no empty spaces next to me
A different day has come I don't feel on my own.

Shannon Groom (12)
Chapter School, Rochester

The Candle

The flame
Flickered as it burnt like ice melting,
The candle
Stood high like a soldier on duty,
Thoughts
Ran through my head like a rapid river,
I feel
Hot and clammy like a beam of light.

It was
Hot enough to melt snow for miles,
Overall
It made me think,
Thoughts
Of pain and sorrow for people in trouble,
Burning
In a heart for a lifetime.

Victoria Moore (12)
Chapter School, Rochester

Them

Quiet, silence all around,
No one speaking or making a sound.

I feel like I am on my own
But I'm not, I'm not, I'm not alone.

My mind is trying to make me speak,
But I know everyone will turn and shriek.

Finally I've done it I've spoken my mind
Now people just want to be unkind.

It's only my opinion, sorry I said it
But no matter what you say I won't regret it.

Georgia-May Hales (12)
Chapter School, Rochester

Christmas

The jingle of bells
The snow crystal-white
The happiness of presents
The Christmas lights so bright
Christmas is warm and joyful.

Children getting excited
Carols being sung
Snowmen being made
Bells being rung
Christmas is for sharing.

Christmas trees put up
Wreaths put on doors
Snowflakes on the windows
Toys sold out in the stores
Christmas is a time for celebrating.

Sonya Hunjan (12)
Chapter School, Rochester

Harvest Festival

The Harvest Festival has come at last!
    But be warned it will go fast.
We give you some food, no need to pay,
    Two words are all you have to say.

I hope you have a lovely year
    No need to shed a tiny tear,
I hope you have a brilliant day,
    I hope you will be OK!

Ending with a friendly smile,
    Walking away from the door,
Starting to walk another mile
    And not caring when your feet get sore.

Charlotte Beaumont-McAllen (12)
Chapter School, Rochester

My Little Broken Heart

I am all alone
Sitting here, doing nothing but thinking of you.
All I see, is a blur right now
While these tears block my view.
All I hear is the laughter,
The laughter we shared those nights
I can feel the wind still blowing through my hair
From the time we sat all through the night.
Just staring up at the sky,
Looking through the stars
You broke my heart
Into two and left me on my own.
While you are free
You let me be
With tears running down my face
And vulnerable to the world.

Ruth Heeney (13)
Chapter School, Rochester

Staring Into Candlelight

The only light of the room,
Was the candlelight disguising the gloom,
The stillness and quietness of the atmosphere,
Gave me thoughts over this year.

The quivering flame of the candlelight,
Stood in the place of the moon at midnight,
With memories and thoughts rushing through my mind,
Relaxed my body on the years behind.

Emily Still (13)
Chapter School, Rochester

Nobody

(Based on the book 'Dear Nobody')

There's something growing inside of me,
Something very small
I call it nobody,
'Cause there's hardly anything at all.

There's something growing inside of me
It's making me very sad,
Chris is suffering as well,
It's looking very bad.

There's something growing inside of me,
Something very small
I don't know if I want it,
I don't know if I want it at all.

Samantha Pugh (12)
Chapter School, Rochester

Own Poem

I have given my heart, I'll even give you my life
But I'll never betray you my love.

My life made such a turning,
I never thought it could have happened.
My love is so much that I can't express it
But I'll throw my life at your feet

Take away my peace
Take away my happiness
And give me all of your grief

I have given my heart; I'll even give you my life
But I'll never betray you my love.

Heenah Akhter (14)
Dormers Wells High School, Southall

Starvation

Starvation is all around the world
Imagine people starving,
No food for them to eat,
No water for them to drink,
Just a pile of bones wrapped in skin

Imagine people dying,
Day after day,
No one to care for them,
No one to bury them

Starving is like a disease,
Never caught
But always killing,
It never helps
But it always kills

Food is precious
But not all can afford it,
It may save lives
But someday will run out.

Huda Khan (14)
Dormers Wells High School, Southall

All Alone

Lying here all alone
No one cares, no one phones.

Wishing I was with someone
Instead of sitting twiddling thumbs.

When will someone realise
Each night tears fill my eyes.

I hope one day someone will know
That I'm sitting here all alone.

Tanya O'Hagan (15)
Dormers Wells High School, Southall

Mother Earth

Oh what wonders has Mother Earth created
The fresh air from the trees that is never hated.

The beautiful flowers that always bloom,
Similar to the lovely moon.

I enjoy watching the sparkling blue sky,
I wish I could go up there and fly.

I also like the big bright sun,
It always makes me happy when I'm feeling glum.

I enjoy the enchanting waterfalls,
Especially when the water calls.

I also like the butterflies that flutter,
I feel happy watching them, when they fly . . . they mutter

Oh what wonders has Mother Earth created.

Rupinder Dhaliwal (11)
Dormers Wells High School, Southall

Someone Once Said

Someone once said that behind every face
There's a story
Like inside every book there's a story
A long story or short story
A happy story or a sad story
And inside every heart there's a light
A bright light or a dim light
What does this really mean and
What does it tell us?
How do we know the stories behind
Each face?
How do we know if we have a
Light in our hearts or not.

Sharon Moti (15)
Dormers Wells High School, Southall

Water Defeats Fire!

Calming blue and relaxing water
Evil red and nasty fire,
Here comes Mrs Jolly's daughter
Looking for someone to hire.

Always telling me to stay away,
But even sometimes washes fire out
Fire always grows again
Without any notice or doubt.

Feeling kind of scared,
Using magical powers washing it out,
Having to be quiet
And never shout.

Water calms people
And never will bend
I'm sorry my guys, this is the *end!*

Rempie Kapoor (12)
Dormers Wells High School, Southall

I Am Unique

In my life I see things that life, can lead me to
Things that I imagine, just like any person would,
But in those hopes I question me . . .
Questions, that I would need innumerable answers to find
I seek for those answers, to find, but only God can I ask,
My mind blends with the thoughts in my mind.
Such thoughts, that no person would find
I cry, but words I can't write,
Because my tears say I,
All I say each tear says my life, my tears say
I am unique I say, unique, that no person would be me.
Then I say, it's alright only patience would pass it by.

Marina Jadran (15)
Dormers Wells High School, Southall

My Eternal Promise To You

You, you are the one,
The one that my heart wants, you are the one.
Where you go,
I will follow you.
Now my life seems like a lifelong punishment without you.
When we become one,
We should dissolve in each other
Like the waves of the deep, wide ocean
Then we should never separate from each other.
That is my eternal promise to you.
You, you are the one,
The one that my heart wants, you are the one.
If I am the voice,
You are my words.
You are dearer to me then the world itself.
When we meet we should never part.
That is my eternal promise to you.
You, you are the one,
The one that my heart wants, you are the one.
If I am the heart
Then you are my heartbeat.
I will hide you in my eyes,
And I will never open my eyes.
You are only mine,
I am only yours.
That is my eternal promise to you.
You, you are the one,
The one that my heart wants, you are the one.
If I am the body,
Then you are the soul.
Love between us is everlasting and you are the only one in my heart
That is my eternal promise to you.

Marvi Lashari (15)
Dormers Wells High School, Southall

The Pain And Struggle

The struggles of a lonely child
He was extremely wild
These are the simple struggles . . .

The lonely child's pains grew
As it went down the drain dew
The only child is all alone
This is the child's pain . . .

As the lonely child grew older
His pain and struggle got colder,
Cries are so futile
This is the boy's troubles . . .

The long life trauma ended
However, the boy's pain and struggle was dreaded
He once was a lonely boy
But found a companion in the shape of a toy . . .

Marlon Farquharson (14)
Dormers Wells High School, Southall

Something Tells You

Something in the bottom of your heart,
Tells you that you are mad,
About what you're not quite sure.
Something tells you that you will do anything,
For what you don't know.
Something tells you that you are in love,
With who you are not sure.

Syrah Ghoier (15)
Dormers Wells High School, Southall

Left To Live

From the day you entered the new world,
Innocent and sin free,
That is the day you arrived in Hell,
Alone. Alone. Just you and me.

We are left to cope
In all the fire
Of jealousy and hate,
Of endless desire.

Why has He left us
To live here alone?
And to stay and face
What is yet unknown?

When are we going to
Go from the pain?
From war, from fighting,
From all the insane?

When are we finally
Going to leave this greed?
Leave every stress behind
That we do not need?

Why is it we have
Only got each other?
Why are we alone
Without any other?

Why is it so hard to survive here?
Why is it so tough?
If this is what my life is, then
I've had *enough!*
Already!

Zubair Ahmad (12)
Dormers Wells High School, Southall

You Never Know What's Going To Happen Tomorrow

Sometimes in your life there is shadows
And sometimes there is sunlight but whatever time
You have spend it with happiness
Because you never know what's going to happen tomorrow.

A person that loves you with all their heart
Is very hard to find, if there is someone like that
Hold their hand and don't let go
Because you never know if that person will be there tomorrow.

Sometimes in life there is shadows
And sometimes there is sunlight but whatever time
You have to spend it with happiness
Because you never know what's going to happen tomorrow.

If you have hurt someone
In whatever way just say sorry
And you'll feel better because you never know
If either of you will be there tomorrow.

Aisha Mohammed
Dormers Wells High School, Southall

My Hometown

Born in Southall, raised in Greenford
A friendly environment and the food, so good
No matter where I go I know where my roots are.
You'll find old buildings but new cars
The community is multicultural
The place is full of bilinguals
We have everything you need,
As well as peaceful parks with evergreen trees.
We all work hard with all our might
Oh well, that's just another day in my life.

Aamna Hussain (12)
Dormers Wells High School, Southall

Always On My Mind

Every day I see you
With your lovely brown eyes
I just want to hold you
And make you mine
If I could have your heart
I sure would love you
I love you more
Than I could love myself
Mountain high or the valley low
You have no idea just how far I'd go.

No matter how far
And no matter how wide
I promise that I'll stay by your side
'Cause in my mind I see you
It's the way you look at me
The sight of you knocks me off my feet
I want to kiss and tell
And get to know you well
Let me introduce my heart to you.

Latoya Wilson (14)
Dormers Wells High School, Southall

Ella

Now you're gone, I feel so sad
But think of the times you made me glad
When we played together and had good fun
In frosty winter and summer sun
You made me laugh, you made me cry
So sad we had to say goodbye
My trusty friend you were so true
And I will always think of you.

Katie Batterbee (11)
Dormers Wells High School, Southall

Nature's Invention

Each day my heart pounds as I see your face
From the first day I saw, the feelings start
Lost love, locked in your heart, I must retrace
My devotion is like a work of art
I feel so lonely without you near me
I crave to have you with me, side by side
I truly believe love can set me free
Mixed emotions run like a funfair ride
And when you are gone, the day drags on by
I wish for you to call, so I can smile
It's enough to make me mad, sad and cry
I'd plead guilty for love, if I'm on trial
You are like an angel, sent from above
Nature's invention made me fall in love.

Sophie Lovelock (15)
Dormers Wells High School, Southall

Darkness

There's a dark place
With an unholy race
In darkness you see an unseen face.

Open his arms to be embraced
Before the rat race
Before monkey had any human traits.

Before the destiny of time and space
In the dark his source was seen
He was tried to be erased
But you might recognise his face
His face is mine to grace.

Danny Ford (14)
Dormers Wells High School, Southall

Who Needs Enemies When You've Got Friends Like These?

Fire burning inside her eyes
Tears of anger flowing out
But somehow nobody notices
They think it's all normal, without a doubt.

Talking about her behind her back
Leaving her out, making her cry
Then suddenly changing to sweet little girls
Every day is a dread, she wishes she could die

She doesn't even mention to anyone,
They wouldn't believe her anyway
Her mouth is aching from pretending to smile
Inside the truth, they're killing her each day.

She doesn't want to be with them
Face the same pain hour after hour
But then whom else does she have?

She has just one question to ask this cruel world
Who needs enemies when you've got friends like these?

Jevanjot Bhinder (13)
Dormers Wells High School, Southall

Grandad

At moments of wonder of you I picture
Beyond the course of countless living years
A gentle breath, a silent glance of peace
Memories are vivid but bereft at present
Awaiting a whisper at every sunrise
Seeking shelter from unknown voices
Sharing thoughts that rise to fill my heart
Thoughts of you and the words you have said
Shall remain a part of me for years
As heavens come forth and wish me life . . .

Masha'al Khan (13)
Dormers Wells High School, Southall

Pegasus

He glides gracefully in elegant flight,
His wings outstretched as he soars through the night,
He is the centre of every child's dreams,
So perfect, so wonderful in everything it seems
The creature of which all are so fond,
And him and elegance form a beautiful bond,
A famous figure in Greek legends, we know . . .
Pegasus . . . Pegasus . . .

He is there - forever - a beautiful winged horse,
Immortality is his of course,
He fills all hearts with passion and love,
Flying high over mountains above,
Swift and silent, night or day,
Not many creatures can equal him this way,
He is unique, special and wonderful . . .
Pegasus . . . Pegasus . . .

Amanda Kumaraiah (11)
Dormers Wells High School, Southall

Nightmares

It was cold,
The house was worn and old
Life was still and plain
I'll never see life again.

It was dark and creepy,
I was cold and sleepy,
I was tired and drained,
I'll never see life again.

The night was dead,
Bad thoughts rushing to my head,
As I woke up in my bed,
I realised I was asleep, not dead!

Ben Coogan (14)
Dormers Wells High School, Southall

Abuse

Here I am on the floor
Lying there motionless next to the door.

I could hear my mum and her friends
Teasing me and calling me all sorts of names

Ssh, here she comes up the stairs
She opens the door and whips me and stares.

She takes some bread out of her pocket and throws it on my bed
'Eat it, eat it now' she stared and she said
'Ssh, here comes my dad'
He opens the door
He shouts all nasty words and says 'You're the reason I am poor'.

Now, here I am nothing to say
Lying here motionless waiting for another day.

Zahra Abbas (13)
Dormers Wells High School, Southall

Animal Squirrel

This animal loves to climb trees,
But doesn't mind if it is followed by fleas
Its body is as small as a ball,
But loves to stand tall.

Its eyes are as big as a bead
And it runs around, as if it's just been freed
Its fur colour is as dull as brown
And its tail is just as round.

It acts as if it's hunting
But likes to act casual by jumping
Its intention is to go around looking for nuts
To fill its family's empty guts.

Julienne Lalong (13)
Dormers Wells High School, Southall

Alone

Questions cloud my head with why
Tears on my pillow as I cry
It's all your fault it's got to be this way
It's the stupid games you play
You've got me upset and confused
Mixed up and bruised
Contemplating should I let you go
Boy why don't you leave me alone
I'm just missing
I'm just wishing
You can give me your reasons
But it won't change my feelings
Through the tears in my eyes
Looking for a reason to replace you
While you walk on by.

Natalie Bolam (15)
Dormers Wells High School, Southall

Life

The sun rises, then sets in the evening
Every day is a different day
But all have a true meaning,
Like what happens or what you get there's nothing you can say.

I dreamt every day for me
It's so different from how I wanted it to be
It's funny how a moment could change your
Life and you don't wanna face what's wrong or right.

There are things in life you just can't
Deny and you can't remove it even if you try.
Life can be cruel with so much pain
I would only face once, never again.

Ranjit Bajwa (14)
Dormers Wells High School, Southall

Stuck In The Middle

Since when have I had my own ambition
And not asked for other people's permission?
You think I can't look after myself
When you have bigger problems yourself
I'm not a little girl
I will grow to understand the world . . .

I don't care what they say
You wait . . . I will get my way
You might as well have your say and mine
Believe me, you will regret all in a few years time
I know it's a challenge; I'm ready for it
My nightmares will burn down, may my dream be lit.

I know it's hard work but bring it on
When I grow up I will prove you all wrong
Seek success, hate the haters
Unlike you, I won't spend life on papers
I will be in control of me
And you cannot stop me from being free.

Sheena Mai (14)
Dormers Wells High School, Southall

Lost Love

Like a damsel in distress, I'm stressing you.
My castle became my dungeon, now I'm longing for you
You're the one that I need to survive
If I can't have you then I'm going to die
My feelings are strong, and still remain
You're my knight in shining armour, you're my saviour
I see your face every night on the silver moon
I just can't let go of that journey of love that once existed.

Amarjit Syan (15)
Dormers Wells High School, Southall

My Life

My life
My life is like a flower
I started off like a seed
Small, helpless and defenceless
But then I started sprouting
Slowly growing, growing
Roots growing veins, growing stronger,
I sprouted beautiful petals
Some days I have good days
When it's sunny and the bees are at work.
I grew into an adult with thorns,
Beautiful yet deadly.
I have a bloodstain-red colour
Not even the heaviest downpour of rain can wash away,
But as I get older I get weaker,
My beautiful petals begin to slowly fall off
And I slowly get ready for my wintered grave
Can you guess what I am?
I am a rose!

Leslie Stevens (14)
Dormers Wells High School, Southall

The Stranger

Lights go off!
Creaks are heard!
Down the corridor
Someone shrieks
Footsteps come closer,
I see a shadow in front of me
I feel a tingling breath upon my neck.
The door slams closed,
As the wind is rushing.
I hear a scream,
My pulse is rushing,
My legs will not move,
I want to run
But . . .
My legs are frozen
Like a lake on Christmas
I see a hand upon my shoulder
I scream, 'Who is it?'

Dimple Gohil (16) & Sonia Mall (15)
Dormers Wells High School, Southall

Why?

I sit and they stare
It's like they really care
I know sometimes I'm really unfair
But I really do care
Why do we act happy?
When we really ain't
Why do we always premeditate
When nothing will change?
Why is it that we always lie and say to?
Make false promises when all we do is just break it?
Sometimes I think we should go our separate ways
But I know we really can't,
We've been through so much
We were almost sisters, now we're bitches
She acts all sweet
I turn my back and then she's talking about me to my closest friends
That's it
I have a solution - let's separate!

Ladan Hussien (14)
Dormers Wells High School, Southall

Black Man's Right

So slavery draws near
Abuse and fights
So many beatings
So many deaths
Judged by race, colour and religion.

From Rosa Parks to Mary Seacole
They risk their lives for a white man
For their rights
Their lives
And families dying for their black life.

I'm proud to be black
Every black man deserves equality
Every black man can walk this Earth's surface
Every black man deserves the respect they should get.

The word 'Black' can mean anything
Black is for respect
Black is for life
Black is for culture
And black is especially for freedom.

Jennifer Ingole (14)
Dormers Wells High School, Southall

Life Is A War

I look above my head, I see the sun shine down
I look around me, the children play in the sun shining down,
I close my eyes in excitement thinking if it's real,
Bang, bang, bang!

Fear runs through my veins,
So much fear I don't want to open my eyes
Things are so much different in fantasy and real life.
Children screaming as if the world has ended,
Don't we all deserve to live till the end?

War is here,
War is there,
War is everywhere,
We are war,
We cause war,
Selfishness makes us use our own humans as an excuse of war,
Think before you act,
Think before you say,
Make a difference, make it now,
We are the feature of this violent world.

Nalab Alaf (14)
Dormers Wells High School, Southall

You Hurt Me Badly

You hurt me . . .
Left me out in the rain . . .
You left me nothing but a lot of memories and pain . . .

I thought you was happy . . .
I thought we would be forever . . .
But I was wrong . . .

How could you say you love me . . . ?
How could this be . . . ?

What happened to our love . . . ?
You left me flat on my face . . .
Poor as a dove . . .

I never cheated or lied . . .
I was there through thick and thin . . .

My feelings have been sold . . .
I wish I was told . . .
I am living in loneliness . . .

I trusted you from my heart . . .
But you tore all apart . . .

Shenika Hogan
Dormers Wells High School, Southall

Flame Of Life

It's only one light
Still so brave and bright
I have been through so much, it's true,
It has been the only thing that has helped me through.

It is my burning desire,
Sometimes it is a raging fire.
Its colours shine through me,
It is the flame of life; our destiny.

Its only wish is for us to carry out our fate,
And to conquer all hate.
The only thing it fears is death,
As it creeps closer with each breath.

I am very ambitious you see,
The flame of life will always burn through me.
The flame is what keeps me going,
It's what keeps my heart beating.

It brightens the darkest night.
Follow it, it is a guiding light
But it will burn you so wickedly, when it doesn't get its way
Teaching you a different lesson with each day.

Chorin Kawa (14)
Dormers Wells High School, Southall

The Mysterious Light

I painted swiftly,
With each brush stroke,
I drew every detail,
Of the colours and the tone.

I looked up to see,
But a flash of light blinded me,
Then I saw it,
An object hitting the sunlight,
That moment was captured,
A shimmering light reflecting of gold,
Still for the time.

The warm colours,
Orange from the horizon, and red from the rose,
Bringing harmony,
Friendliness, warmth, peace and joy.

I have that moment
Kept safely in my heart,
It will be with me every day
And I shall never forget it
As long as I live,
For it is a mystery of what it was.

Manveer Bhullar (12)
Dormers Wells High School, Southall

I Would Let You Know!

Time will say nothing but I told you so
Time only knows the price we have to pay,
If I could tell you I would let you know.

If we should weep when clowns put on their show,
If we should stumble when musicians play,
Time will say nothing but I told you so.

There are no fortunes to be told, although,
Because I love you more than I can say,
If I could tell you I would let you know.

The winds must come from somewhere when they blow
There must be reasons why the leaves decay;
Time will say nothing but I told you so.

Perhaps the roses really want to grow,
The vision seriously intends to stay;
If I could tell you I would let you know.

Suppose the lions all get up and go,
And all the brooks and soldiers run away;
Will time say nothing but I told you so?

If I could tell you, I would let you know.

Malcolm Lancaster (14)
Dormers Wells High School, Southall

Do You Love Me

The other day I thought you would say the 3 important words,
'I love you,'
I truly need to know for sure.
Do you love me the way I love you?

Love, love, love
Is this what you feel for me?
Love, love, love
Can I be your only girl?

There's something special about you,
Everyone else sees it too,
The way your beautiful eyes shine like stars,
Are you the hunk sent from Mars?

Love, love, love
That's what should keep us together forever,
Love, love, love
You know I love you more than anything else in the world.

Remember when we first met,
We couldn't take our eyes off each other,
So you know how I feel about you,
Please just tell me you feel the same way too!

Amrit Sangha (14)
Dormers Wells High School, Southall

Promises

You broke all those promises that we once made,
You made me feel that I had been betrayed.
I thought we were going to last forever,
But it seems to me, you thought we were never.

All those times you said you loved me,
To your heart, you said I was the key.
You said I was perfect, you said I was the one,
Then all of a sudden, you were gone.

Where did you go? Why did you go?
If there was a problem, you should have let me know
Where did you go? Why did you go?
Just answer these few questions I want to know.

You knew that to fix us, I would try,
You knew I didn't like seeing you cry.
But I don't understand why you looked in my eyes,
And made those promises which were just lies.

If you were going to leave,
Why in your 'false' love did I believe?
Maybe it was the way you said
Our love would never end.

Umarah Ahmad (14)
Dormers Wells High School, Southall

Darkness The Curse

In the darkness
Darkness leers
Swifting lightly
God knows where.

Catching light
Heaven's here
Angels near.

Curse those dreams
They haunt me here
The everlasting fear
The grow of terror

The dreams that come every night
Scare me there
Scare me here
Scare me every day
Every minute of the day.

Let the dreams go away
Just like the wind on a summer's day
The light of life
From the night light
My best friend
That saves me from this curse.

Sukhvinder Basran (14)
Dormers Wells High School, Southall

My Heart's Only Desire . . .

My heart's only desire . . .
Was to share my dreams with you . . .

You were my love, my life, my everything
Yet you still broke my heart,
Destroyed it in two and left me with nothing.

You meant the world to me
Together forever I just wanted us to be
We could have even made dreams come true
But guess things didn't go well though.

Boy all I ever do is think about you
Why don't you understand I really need you?
Please come back to me cos it's overdue
And at least tell me you love me too.

Look into my eyes
For once realise
Without you my soul dies
My heart it bleeds and for only you it cries.

You shattered my dreams
And now you don't care is how it seems
Thinking about you sends shivers up and down my spine
Although deep down I know you were never mine.

Sophia Khan (14)
Dormers Wells High School, Southall

My Bed

My alarm clock's shrill scream calls me from slumber,
Proclaiming the time in flashing numbers.
I don't want to get up and go to school,
Or venture into the world so harsh and cruel.
I don't want to get up,
I'd rather instead stay safe in the warm,
In my warm, cosy bed.

I shiver and yawn as my maths teacher old,
Keeps me awake in my classroom so cold.
I don't want to do all of these difficult sums,
I can hardly wait till home time comes.
I don't want to be here, I'd rather instead,
Be at home in the warm in my wonderful bed.

My mother points a tyrannical finger,
To the door but I still linger.
My Xbox sits idle, calling my name,
Begging me to play just one more game.
I'm forced to give in, though I'd rather instead,
Stay up and play games than go to my,
Awful,
Horrible,
Cold,
Bed!

Jessica Murray (12)
Dormers Wells High School, Southall

The Special Month

Place yourself in the position of the poor,
Feel the hunger attacking you more and more.

Learn to be patient
Learn to forgive,
Feed the nation,
Who all want to live.

Feel very spiritual,
Peaceful and calm
This holy month is special
It's Ramadan.

Families get together
To feast on the delicious food
Feeling united forever,
Excluding the meaning of rude.

Do something powerful,
Make yourself proud
Fill your heart with love
Show the world out loud.

It's the time of the year
Where the gates of Heaven are there
So don't follow what you hear,
Let's all be proud, don't you think it's fair?

Zainab Mosa (14)
Dormers Wells High School, Southall

The Day In The Park

I was in the park
Sitting on a swing
Lonely and quiet, without a single thing
The wind had started to howl
The dog started to growl
The sky was looking glum
As I started to bite my thumb.

Along came this beautiful girl
Whistling all her way, eating a twirl
She sat down beside me, making me feel shy
My mouth swelled up and went all dry
I was trying to say something but nothing came out
I was speechless and empty, without a single shout
She stared at me for a second or so
As the wind got fierce and started to blow.

Her face had made my heart beat fast
As if I was in a race and about to come last
Her eyes made my stomach go funny
She looked so sweet, just like a bunny
Her hair was soft and so straight
I was dying to ask her out on a date
So then she left, walking her way
Me being a fool had an awful day.

Faisal Ali (13)
Dormers Wells High School, Southall

Then The Morning Comes

The wind roared
The night soared
That night dream
Could hear a scream
The trees rustled
The people bustled
Then comes the morning
It hears my mourning
Where the bird hums
We stand glum
Down my cheeks the tears trickle
The body stings
And the fingers prickle
The water falls
Those four men stand tall
Carrying the corpse with them
And stop those four men
The ground has been dug
And the person is lowered
So that it fits in snug
The earth is wet
With fear I sweat
I wish it could've been me
With me even cries the sea.

Madeeha Ahmed (15)
Dormers Wells High School, Southall

Street Life

What's with all the violence? What's with all the crime?
Enjoy life while you can,
Stop wasting time
What's with all the shooting? What's with all the guns?
Every time you pull one out,
Someone's life is done.
What's with all the ecstasy? What's with all the drugs?
All it does is lead you to becoming a thug.
What's with all the fighting? What's with all the beats?
When someone sees you doing it,
Everyone repeats.

I see people walking streets, from day to day
I've seen more people being led astray
All they can do now is to pray
Before their life is forced away.

People always end up getting hurt
They always end up being upset and scared in their heart
I don't like a person who hates and deceives
They've always got tricks up their sleeves
Pain is felt everyday in a mind and in a heart
It's like a shock; it's felt like a spark
Maybe happiness will be found
Until then they'll look around.

Debbi Sukul (13)
Dormers Wells High School, Southall

21st Century Definition Of Beauty

Let her hair be of dark colour,
Resembling the darkness of the blackberry
Let her hair be of a spherical shape,
Her eyebrows thin and not hairy.

Let there be a path of a golden colour,
Between the twins of night.
Let her have a spherical heat that
Fits perfectly into her hair.

Her nose straight and not crooked
Her nose neither too long nor too short
Pampered and treated,
Bringing it up to perfection.

Let her eyes be of a dangerous, dark black
Her teeth white as snow
Her lips soft, thin and flamboyant
Let her long, thin arms be soft and gentle,
Leading to their elegant, thin fingers
Be her legs of a short, thin and delicate nature
And so it is to the toes they lead to.

Let her body structure be of glee,
Showing the 21st Century definition of beauty
As described by me.

Nigel Madinga (13)
Dormers Wells High School, Southall

Lost Dream

Remember last summer
When you and I were close?
The bond between us was so strong,
I thought you were forever.
I'll always remember,
Your sweet smile and those eyes.
It was that seaside town,
That brought us together.
Now that we are back,
We have grown apart.
All I have is memories,
They are becoming so distant now.
We were living in a dream,
Where everything was possible.
That dream is now gone,
But it should have stayed.
I want that dream back,
It broke my heart to see it fade.
I had so much love,
I can't let it go.
I doubt that I will love anyone as much as you.
Here I am now, trying to stand strong,
Desperately holding onto the memory.
All I have left to say is,
'I love you and can't forget!'

Vanessa Vera (16)
Dormers Wells High School, Southall

We Came A Long Way

Here is where we live
But not where we come from
So much we have achieved
Since we were made to leave our home.

So much we have lost
So many awful cries
We fought but to the cost
Of seeing our own people die.

Hard, we worked for liberty
A chance to defeat the enemy
All we wanted was equality
A chance to live in harmony.

So yes, my people
Be proud of who you are
For you have achieved it all
Even when times were hard.

Long may be the road
And high the mountain top
But still we march forward
And we know we will not stop
Until the glorious day
When all our troubles will fly away
And we will finally be able to say
We made it! We came a long way!

Charlene Badibanga (14)
Dormers Wells High School, Southall

Nightmares

When you least expect it,
It comes in your head,
While in your joyful sleep,
In your comfy bed.

And when it comes,
That is it,
It makes you scared,
Till the night is lit.

All those scary things
Fly round in your mind,
Like a tornado of terror,
As you will find.

It makes you pant,
It makes you sweat,
It makes you scream
And makes you jet off the bed.

You run in the corridor,
But it stretches so wide,
It makes you feel
Like you've run a million miles.

But as you run they're chasing you,
All those creepy eeky scares,
And that is how it sadly feels,
Those things that you call *nightmares!*

Zeshaan Iqbal (13)
Dormers Wells High School, Southall

I Am A Thinker

I like to think
I think of yesterday
I think of today
I think of tomorrow
But, I don't like to think of sorrow.

I like to think of you
I like to think of me
I like to think of us
My thinking never ends.

I think life is like a lift
It has its ups and downs
I think life is a gift.

I think of war
I think of peace
I think of faith
I think these are no more.

I think I am sane
I think I am mad
I think I am happy
But sometimes I may be a little sad.

I like to think
So I think I am a thinker
Sometimes I think deep
Sometimes I think even deeper
So in conclusion, I think I am a thinker.

Chandni Dhakal (14)
Dormers Wells High School, Southall

The Error In Our Love

I look outside in the darkness
Wishing you were here in my arms,
I reminisce about the times we had

And the ways you and me were charmed.
What went wrong in this relationship?
I felt we were meant to be,
My emotions for you were never pretence
But over time they sealed.
Later I saw you once or twice.

My heart began to ache,
I looked at you and saw the guy I loved,
My back spun the other way
When I was around you, it felt so unreal
The complications, the memories, began to reveal;
I can't believe you didn't see
That our past love is destroying me.

Maybe if you were quick to declare
What you had felt for me
Today we wouldn't be so far apart
Relying on our destiny.

Now again I'm challenging my luck
Hoping you'll forget the past,
Think of me as the girl you once loved,
And maybe
Just maybe . . . this time we'll last.

Uzma Saleem (15)
Dormers Wells High School, Southall

My Mother Country

A pearl resting on the Indian Ocean,
Always being licked by waves,
Never has it been discovered,
But it's a paradise destroyed by war.

Oh, how I'd like to go back,
Sit on my window sill,
And admire its beauty,
While the sun glares at my back.

Oh, how I'd like to sit in my garden,
While the rain touches my body
And hugs me with its icy fingers
And blows its cold breath on my face.

Oh, how I'd like to sit on the sand
Watching the waves running towards me
And returning in dismay
And that noise of the wind,
Which oozes into my skin.

Oh, how I'd like to sit on a tree,
Hugging myself with a blanket
Looking at the gigantic mountains,
Which dominates the whole city.

Oh, how I'd love to see the busy roads,
Crowded by people and vehicles,
The dust, the smell, the heat, the noise,
All pouring down on me.

I'll be back, Sri-Lanka, I'll be back!

Janani Arulrajah (13)
Dormers Wells High School, Southall

My Love . . .

Love, love, mysterious love
My love's as sweet as air
It floats around like fluffy clouds
Or pieces of loose hair
My love for you will never fade
You can always count on me
I love you so my sweetie cake
As much as you love me.

You talk to me in many ways
You never lose your cool
You give me stuff like candy bars
Or caramel liqueur.

Your teeth as white as paper
Your hair's as black as mine
Your skin is like a golden star
That shines upon the night
You love to play my games
And hang around with me
You always walk me to my door
And kiss me on the cheek.

I love the way you dress
And the way you cut your hair
I love the way you make me laugh
When I'm sitting on the stairs
I'll be there for you
And you'll be there for me
As long as we keep each other
For the rest of eternity.

Leonie Thomas (14)
Dormers Wells High School, Southall

A Love That's Never Been Seen

Love's deep dark desire,
Is a long lasting fire.

You're my only guiding star,
But why are we always so far?

You showed me how to love,
Are you a spiritual dove?

We spend so much time apart,
Instead you could just say that your heart,

Has a deep, dark desire,
If it's not true call me a liar.

There's something in you that I didn't see before,
Tell me so I can rest assure.

We're so close at heart,
There's no need for us to restart.

There's something that you crave,
Tell me and be brave.

If your love is blessed,
Then why am I so depressed?

Tell me once again my dear,
What is it that you fear?

Is it the love that you never had
Or the time that you were sad?

You're my king,
And I'm your queen,

Together we can be a love that's never been seen.

Mohammed Abbas (14)
Dormers Wells High School, Southall

Love Is Nice!

Love is nice,
But as sharp as a knife,
At times as quiet as mice.

Love is joy,
Made for both girl and boy,
It is given even to a toy.

Love can be bad,
Addictive as a drug, when it starts as a bud,
And terminates with a thud.

One without love is vacant,
One's dreams are ditched,
Their feelings are untouched.

The symbol of love is a heart
To show when it starts,
The sign of its end is lightning,
Nothing much frightening.

But never have you minded, because love is nice,
It is the summer breeze,
Like the winter chill,
Yet it may shed like the leaves off a tree in autumn,
When it loses colour,
However, love has harmony like the singing of birds in spring.

Love is a heart
But very sweet
When two hearts meet
Love is complete.

Aneesa Mohammed (15)
Dormers Wells High School, Southall

Black In The Day

Black in the day
We were slaves
For slaves had to be brave
Pain came hour by hour
Sweet life they each devoured
Work got tough, no time for laughs
Tear droplets of desire.

Black in the day
We prayed
For life was unhappily made
Back in time
We maintained the right mind
To each other Blacks were kind
Now praying is used for confession
So we are not left in depression
As Jesus walks, our preacher talks
And shows us the flame of freedom.

Black in the day
Our solution was prayer
As our owners, just didn't care
Back then we prayed for hope
Now all some do is pray for dope
For freedom our owners said nope!
At each other's throat, killing is now a sport
For our world of wonders
Is rapidly turned
For now our world is wicked.

We all now need a wing of wisdom
For eye of envy has polluted our system
Think of the children affected they'll be
Like damaged rose petals floating swiftly on sea
On each lay down your problems and fears
This is our opportunity
Start as one like we first begun
Build back our broken community.

Kirstie Jones (14)
Dormers Wells High School, Southall

Man Utd Are The Best!

Man Utd are the best,
Better than the rest,
I support them every day,
So victory is on their way.

When they're on the football pitch,
Their heads are held up high,
When my team are thrashing them,
They always shout out 'Why?'

My favourite player is Van Nistelrooy
When he scores a goal,
We all have joy,
Then when my team has won the game,
They'll all come back to do the same.

Man Utd are the best,
Better than all the rest,
I support them every day,
So victory is on their way.

Chandni Fatania (11)
Dormers Wells High School, Southall

Friendship Is . . .

Friendship is a rainbow spreading through the sky
Friendship is funny, laughing until you cry
Friendship is a tiny plant, getting better as it grows
Friendship is just knowing what the other knows
Friendship is sticking together; no one can get between you
Friendship is accepting something or someone new
Friendship is loyal, strong, fun and tough
Friendship is friendship
I think I've said enough.

Laura Cox (13)
Enfield County School, Enfield

Evil

Evil has always been there
With eyes of stone and very, very pale skin,
He holds a devil's fork,
He has a cauldron
He has huge, tall horns
And when he is near
I feel red-hot fire.

Evil has always been here
I can hear swords clashing,
A burning cauldron,
A screaming child,
I feel when he's near, fear,
Bright lights turning dark.

Evil has always been here
He looks at me as if he's about to kill,
As if to stab,
As if to murder,
Blood is on the dance floor,
Blood is on the knife
I see a dead person
I hear a child screaming.

Evil has always been here,
I feel like a criminal has struck me
A smooth criminal,
I hear police sirens,
Banging around in my head
Evil has always been here,
And that's what he said.

Laura Fredericks (13)
Enfield County School, Enfield

Jealousy

You're here
You're there,
You're everywhere I look.
What are you?

You're the cloudy sky,
The rainy day,
The evil grin,
And sarcastic smile.

You're on my side but destroy my life,
I turn to look at you but you're not there,
You're her new trainers,
His new car
I wish I knew just what you are!
You're not a person,
Not a thing,
But you're something
Something inside me!

You're what only I can see,
With huge, round eyes,
The brightest green,
I look at you,
You look at me,
The thing is . . . only I can see . . .

Bronwen Davies (13)
Enfield County School, Enfield

Fear

Fear is like a war waiting to happen
Like the feeling ghosts and ghouls are under the bed
Fear is like a little child sitting in his room scared of the dark
Fear is like being out with your friends
And thinking someone's following you
Like a wolf lurking in the bushes, waiting to jump out.
The noise of an owl, a dentist's drill
And the heavy breathing of a killer,
Fear,
Stays there,
Won't go
Forever.

Rebecca Barrowcliffe (13)
Enfield County School, Enfield

Werewolf In A Dungeon

The werewolf hunted in agony
Tormented for blood
In the nightmare
Panic, terror, suffering
In the midnight
The monster screeched in shock
In horror, fright and gloom
Its spirit was tortured
Its dungeon was in darkness
Dread and death
Until it died
And was put in its grave.

Stuart Anderson (12)
Furness Special School, Swanley

Monster Munch

Moaning monster munch
On your bones he likes to crunch
You will make a tasty lunch
If you're fat you'll be a tasty brunch
Stay away, follow your hunch.

While he's weeping
You will be sure to be shrieking
Your bones are chilling
While he's feeding
A doctor you will be needing.

Harry Ramsden (13)
Furness Special School, Swanley

Autumn

It was a scary night
On Grasswood Common
The children were all asleep
The trees along the field were bristling
And their leaves were falling off.

John Moorcroft (13)
Furness Special School, Swanley

Motorbike - Haiku

Racing down dirt fields
It sounds good when you change gear
Feels like you're flying

Lee May (14)
Furness Special School, Swanley

Wolf Fight

There they stand all alone in the moonlight
Preparing for battle at an hour of night
Two wolves face each other with teeth gleaming bright,
Their eyes glazed over, they are preparing to fight.

One leaps for the other, his claws razor-sharpened,
One is attacking, one tries to defend,
Slashing, gashing, howling and barking
Claws are flying, razor-sharpened.

At last the fight has finally finished
There a corpse laid, a foe diminished
The victor is bleeding and is scarred for life
Stands to the creatures that watched the fight.

He howls to the moon and falls to the ground
All the creatures gathered around,
His soul passes into the damned,
His body disappears not a trace could be found.

All heard the angel of death speak,
'I'm taking him now, I'm taking him deep.'

James Ruane (13)
Furness Special School, Swanley

Ghosts

Ghost cemetery
Phantoms haunting, screeching graves
Poltergeists creeping

In the ghastly cemetery
Midnight approaching
The ghosts are waking
Tortured souls are screaming!

Quick get out, before you are savagely murdered.

Dominic Glen (13)
Furness Special School, Swanley

Bats' Fright Night

Bats who live in the church's steeple
At night come out to frighten people
The fear you feel, unspeakable
Bats who live in the church's steeple.

Bats who live in high places
At night cover your faces
They will follow your paces
Bats in high places.

Bats hex the dawn of the dead
At night take care to cover your head
Bloodthirstily they wait to be fed
Bats hex the dawn of the dead.

Bats bite when they come out at night
Bats come out to fright at night
Bats make your skin feel all tight
Bats bite when they come out at night.

Bats are nervous, scared of people
That's why bats hide in the church's steeple
To kill a bat is quite unspeakable
Bats are nervous, scared of people.

Sam Cabassi (13)
Furness Special School, Swanley

Love

Red is the colour of love
Red is the colour of Valentine roses
Blue is the colour of your eyes.

Red is the colour of a winter jumper
Red is the colour of cold blood
Red is the colour of Mars
Red is the colour of your eyes when angry.

Karl Capon (11)
Furness Special School, Swanley

Making It Back

Staggering through the desert,
The scorching sun deliberating,
Hiding in bushes,
The sound of travellers,
The intense heat,
Sweat running down our faces,
'Is there hope?'

The youngest stumbling behind,
Stony, sun-baked earth, jagged, crumbling rocks,
Her feet cut, aching and swollen.
Faces drop, a sandstorm,
Huddled together, their panic-stricken faces,
Sand swarming around them, blinding them,
'What do we do?'

Carrying on through the desert, deeper and deeper,
Weak and dehydrated,
A waterhole lies in front of them,
Their faces fill with joy,
A sound high up in the air,
It's the spirit bird flying around them,
'There is hope!'

Sumayya Merali (12)
Northwood College, Northwood

Rabbit-Proof Fence

Walking through the desert,
Hour after hour,
Not seeing a thing,
No sign of vegetation,
Not even a flower.

They are coming, so run,
Almost out of breath,
I am blinded by the sun,
Hide behind a rock.

I look down at my sock,
Blood is on my feet,
They are sore,
I can't walk, I need help.

I need to get to the fence,
I need to see my family,
These people do not make sense.
What have we done wrong?
Wait! I can hear the song!

Nearly here!
We wish they were gone.
We need to be saved,
I don't want to grow up
Being their slaves.

Stephanie Bryan-Kinns (12)
Northwood College, Northwood

Sonnet

Summer:

Look at the beautiful sun in the sky,
Shining and twinkling like a bright star.
Look high, at the colourful birdies fly,
Sit in a quiet place, not in a car.
In the night look at the wonderful moon,
Watch the moon fade away and the sun come.
Listen carefully at day, night and noon,
The quietest place is at night, at home.
Let the animals all sleep peacefully,
Make no noise and let us not disturb it.
Walk in the park, play about carefully,
Run about, skip along, make yourself fit.
Use a fan because it is hot and warm,
This is summer, at least there is no harm.

Charleen Sylvian-Shantaruban (12)
Northwood College, Northwood

The Golden Oldies

Some people tend to disrespect the old,
We mustn't forget they are precious like gold.
Surely the elderly believe that is so,
We have to appreciate how much they know.
Often they're treated as though they were babes,
As we put them in homes, we don't realise,
That they have feelings too and just maybe,
They are not old through someone else's eyes.
In nursing homes they may be neglected,
Being old truly should not be a crime.
Society makes them feel rejected,
But they know we all will be old in time.

As we treat the old, so may we be treated,
Because history tends to be repeated.

Georgina Dunlop (12)
Northwood College, Northwood

The Snow

The snowflakes fall upon the crunchy snow,
They shine and sparkle on the mountain top,
The snow has little footprints of a crow,
They land, hitting the ground with a loud *plop*.

They stream into the puddle lethargically,
One by one they all melt away silently,
Being careful not to slip into the pool,
They rush again to the top of Mount Icy.

Skiing through lumpy snow looking for holes,
They won't disturb anything being nice.
I see the sun appearing through the snow's soul,
Dying restlessly with cracks in the ice.

But I'm sure they'll come back one snowy day,
They'll come back one day when the snow is out.

Nikita Shah (12)
Northwood College, Northwood

My Dog, Jack

My true best friend on Earth is my dog, Jack.
He guards and protects me wherever I go.
He loves to chase cats, white, brown, sand or black
And loves to bury his face in the snow.
He's soft and cuddly with a red and white coat,
But we take pity on his mournful face.
He loves to paddle, but dislikes our boat,
When we first met, he ran after my lace.
He's a rascal when it comes to food
And has been caught eating a birthday cake.
He's a lovely dog, but can be quite rude,
Because of the mega farts he doth make!
He's still lively, although he's getting old,
But can bite the postman's bum if he's feeling bold!

Helena Lewczynska (12)
Northwood College, Northwood

The Doves And The Children

The doves flew swiftly through the winter's day,
As fast as the children could hold on tight.
The doves dived through the nights of windy May,
As they shuffled for food in the bright light.

The doves chased the children, who played in sand,
They began to run as fast as they chewed.
The doves flew faster until they had to land,
The children ran and started to chuck food.

Swooping through the trees, the doves found a key,
The children stopped at a halt to eat food.
Diving into a turquoise, cold, blue sea,
The children followed the doves in a mood.

The doves flew as happily as they could,
The children went to bed as they should.

Monal Shah (12)
Northwood College, Northwood

The Wicked Woman

She died all alone, the wicked old lady,
Hated by everyone and everything,
She was known to be extremely crazy,
As she killed all the children with an awful 'ping'.
Only a few children ever ran free,
Once she had them, there was nothing they could do,
But those who escaped were stung by her bee
And then they would never know who was who.
The villagers tried time and again to kill her as best they could,
But try as they might, the wicked woman won.
Despite the fact they knew very well they should,
But they were forced to wait till her time was done.
In all, one hundred children were killed,
By such a wicked woman whose stomach was filled.

Jessica Lancod-Frost (12)
Northwood College, Northwood

The Journey

Trackers chase us through the desert
Across the long, cracked plain
Through the river, up stream not down
Along the rabbit-proof fence

The baking sun on our blistering feet
The motionless trees out of our reach
The tiring footsteps in the twilight
The silence of the hot, dry night

Dust suspended in the air
Water is needed so off we go
Sand stirring around our toes
The ground embracing us as we sleep the night

Nine weeks without a roof
All the time spent alone
We lose our cousin but we must not moan
Relief overcomes us as we are welcomed home.

Charlotte Rome (12)
Northwood College, Northwood

The Autumn

What is autumn? The harvesting season.
The days get colder, ready for winter,
The old russet leaves, that is the reason,
Bringing the firewood, don't get a splinter!
The leaves on the trees are slowly changing,
At least the autumn sun is still shining!
The leaves turn red from green that are fading,
Harvests, orchards, preparation timing.
Summer, it seems a lifetime away,
The robins are now coming here to sing,
Autumn colours make a beautiful day,
The swallows are now flying on the wing.
The flowers are dead and everything's grey,
For this is autumn, that's all I can say.

Reena Shah (13)
Northwood College, Northwood

The Mighty Spirit Bird

The bird from afar,
The bird from near,
We shall not fear.

For we have the spirit bird,
Though it may seem absurd.
He soars through the sky,
The stunning sight passing by,
His beautiful beak and wings,
His beak through which he gracefully sings.

The spirit bird is always here,
His job is to look after the dear.
Always looking from above,
Like a sweet, caring dove.
Flying higher than any other,
Also further than any other.

The bird from afar,
The bird from near,
Whom we shall not fear.

Meera Bhudia (13)
Northwood College, Northwood

Looking For Home

The blazing sun beating
On the dry, cracked earth,
Burning their blistered feet,
Helplessly gasping for water and shade,
But the trees were motionless and dying.
The three isolated, dying,
The intensity is too much, dragging across the sand,
Forming patterns,
But they fail, falling to the ground.
Going into a deep sleep forever . . .
Never to be awakened.

Meera Shah (12)
Northwood College, Northwood

The Australian Desert

The Australian desert, full of life,
This is where I call home.
Where the skies are orange at sunrise,
Blue at midday
And a beautiful pink at sunset.
I wish I was at home.

I loved that place. So fresh.
A cool breeze blew through my face.
I miss my mum. Her soul, so happy.
I wish I was back at home. Near the fence.
But now I am here.
I wish I was at home.

The white people took me away from my family.
My mum was crying.
'Where are you taking her?' she yelled.
I had no answer for her.
I'm here at the camp.
I wish I was at home.

They checked the colour of my skin.
Mr Neville said that I am an unfortunate case.
He said that there was too much black in me.
I heard them say that they need to get rid of the black.
They are strict and they are harsh.
I wish I were at home.

I tried to escape.
This time I was successful.
The sun was hot but I kept going.
I wasn't that far away from my home.
I could hear my mother's singing.
I was at home.

Ishleen Kaur (12)
Northwood College, Northwood

Australia

Dry, hot and yellow,
Is the Australian land.
But cooler it gets,
As night draws in.

The sand baking,
Gets cool and stirs.
The motionless trees and leaves,
Get swaying and rustling.
The orange, sunlit sky,
Turns deep, midnight blue.
The blazing sun beating on the dry earth,
Turns to the moon guiding the animals.
The deserted land with no one about,
Turns into a parade of animals by sunset.

The fish in the warm water,
Come out of the weed to feed.
The crocodiles bathing in the mud,
Lift themselves up slowly,
Hoping to catch some prey.

The kangaroos hop,
The cuddly koalas sleep.
The birds in their nests,
Soar in night-time breeze.

The stars glow,
The moon shines,
Leading the animals back home.
The sun rising again,
To see no life about,
Not having the slightest clue,
About what went on through the night.

Dipali Amin (12)
Northwood College, Northwood

The Spirit Bird Prayer

Never fear,
The spirit bird is here.
He will help you,
No matter what.

He will guide you,
In the moonlit night.
Whatever happens,
He'll be by your side.

That's what my mother said
And now I'm in danger.
Won't you come and rescue me?
Because I need your help.

Why is Mr Devil
So cunning and mean?
Why don't we do something
To demolish this scheme?

Who is this ghost lady,
Escorting me to our room?
I'm ever so frightened
Won't you take me home?

Never fear,
The spirit bird is here.
He will help you,
No matter what.

He will guide you,
In the moonlit night.
Whatever happens,
He'll be by your side.

Reshma Dhamecha (12)
Northwood College, Northwood

The Ocean Sonnet

Around the world, the ocean shines so blue,
Sometimes beams a shade of emerald green,
The ocean makes the sand sticky like glue,
But then you wash yourself and put on cream.

In every ocean mammals live and fish,
Only few mammals live in the ocean,
People like to eat fish on a clean dish,
Children use the ocean to make potions.

There are mammals like the whales and dolphins,
They like to eat fish like heron and shrill,
Dolphins can be sown with the help of pins,
To eat shrill, the whales must get quite a thrill.

This sonnet is all about the ocean,
So don't forget to put on your lotion.

Priya Uka (12)
Northwood College, Northwood

The Australian Desert

Stretching, reaching along the plain,
Sand upon sand, no sight of rain,
The heat from the sun, no ease from the pain,
If the sun doesn't stop, you'll go insane.

There are no animals around you,
Nothing here to eat or drink,
Not even a little cuckoo,
Or even a lizard skink.

Golden yellow, orange, red,
The sand's colours, like a coloured bed,
All you need is a place to rest your head,
You really need to be fed.

Caroline Perkins (13)
Northwood College, Northwood

The Europeans' Arrival In Australia

We dragged our horses across the dusty dunes,
Our feet on fire,
Our supplies run out,
Death waiting eagerly to devour us all.
Call for help and the echo calls back,
Explorers survive storms and raging seas,
But not isolation,
This strange land was a death plantation.
So we waited as twilight fell,
Brilliant colours lit up the sky,
Death cackled,
Stretching its claws and engulfing us one by one.
The last thing we saw was a strange beast,
Watching us while a bird looked at me with its beady eyes.
I heard the last squawk of a bird and I was gone.

Laura Smith (12)
Northwood College, Northwood

Sensations To Be Found

The smooth sensation was running through my fingers,
The glistening sand oozing through the gaps of my hand.
The sun kissing the grass made me want to gasp,
The dingoes' trails made monstrosity invalid for,
The sun priding for me.

The picture was sweet, the picture was calm,
Until the massacre of scorpions arrived.
The sun fell down onto the ground
And slaughter struck.
What bad luck.
My feet murdered the sand,
The gentle vibration crammed.
Where shall I go?

Aarthi Jegatheeswaran (12)
Northwood College, Northwood

The Snow

The crystal snowflakes light the charcoal sky,
The whistling wind swims swiftly in the air,
Curious ants watching the sky ask why,
Milk-coloured stones hit them without a care.

Like icing on a cake, the snow covers,
A shadowed pavement and all the sadness,
More tears of God fly down with the others
And merrily twirl like ballerinas.

Out of their window joyful children see,
With their animated eyes widening,
A view that leaves their faces full of glee,
Their cheeks the colour of the sun rising.

But like the sun which at night fades away,
This snow scene does not last eternally
And unfortunately, by the next day,
There was no snow for their eyes left to see.

All that's left of the snow is memories,
That circle our minds like a gentle breeze.

Sara Asaria (12)
Northwood College, Northwood

The Desert Haikus

The desert's sun beams
The burning, sandy desert
Hungry to see life

The motionless trees
Deserted, dry and cracked earth
Blistering sand stirs

No strength to go on
The midnight-blue, twilight sky
Unpredictable.

Yasmin Patel (12)
Northwood College, Northwood

Is This Autumn?

The sky is blue, the clouds are white and grey
The wind blows all the leaves upon the trees
Although we are not in the month of May
I wonder why that is what I do see.

The days are short, the nights become so long
The clocks go back and we acquire an hour
Which can for some at first seem very wrong
The leaves on trees die, autumn has the power.

Some animals hibernate cos of cold
People buy warm clothes for this new season
Most people do because their clothes are old
They will have their own personal reasons.

Well is this true? What do you think of it?
Autumn may be coming. Do you have the kit?

Emma Teboul (14)
Northwood College, Northwood

The Moonlight

I see up high, the moon on this dark night,
Twinkling stars in the dazzling sky,
Shooting stars zooming right and left with might,
Lonely tramps on this cold night close one eye,
The snow falls beautifully to the ground,
One or two cars patrol the empty street,
Elegant swans peacemaking all around,
The fires in the houses giving off heat,
Two playing outside - a father and daughter,
People shivering in the cold night air,
Lovers still strolling in the park cuddle,
Snow falls heavily, another snow pair,
Two dogs playing and splashing in puddles,
Night is so nonchalant when there's no rain,
So see you darkness, I'll see you again!

Alexa Fitzpatrick (12)
Northwood College, Northwood

Rain

All the fresh rain that falls upon the ground,
Soaks all the kids walking along the road,
It will turn all the mud into a mound,
And out from all the bushes come the toads.

The rain will flood all of the London streets,
When it rains the people will stay inside,
Because it drowns the places people meet,
Animals have to go away and hide.

Life feels like it stops outside when it rains,
All the roads fill themselves with big puddles,
The rain will make your body full of pains,
The weathermen get themselves in muddles.

Everything looks wet when the rain stops,
Even when it has rained on the big rocks.

Rosie Griggs (13)
Northwood College, Northwood

The Robin

The robin sits on his branch quietly
He starts to draw breath slowly now
He starts to let out a whistle slowly
It's starting to get louder here - wow!
You can see his fiery red breast clearly
His feathers look so pretty - brown and fluffy
He is singing his song, not very shy
He is small and beautifully puffy
He spreads his red and blue wings proudly now
He starts to flap his wings, see them flap, flap
He starts to soar through the sky smoothly - wow!
He is flying without a clue, no map
He falls to the ground, he has spotted worms
He pulls out one of the worms and eats it.

Rebecca Bingham (12)
Northwood College, Northwood

Unrequited Love

I am at a loss to describe the sight
It was too easy to run and play
But you do not seem to feel my plight
But only looked to run away
If only it was simple to choose
Then for me there could only be you
Instead it was my turn to lose
Oh, how could I not be blue?
I am sure you know what I mean
As I sit here and sigh
For you have shown you are not so keen
So all I can say is goodbye
        Is this what it has come to for me?
        All I ask is for you to hear my plea.

Alexandra Kleist-Patchett (13)
Northwood College, Northwood

The Dalmatian Of My Dreams

Look upon my swift Dalmatian hound,
Standing here with head held high and proud.
Then off he goes across the open ground,
He thinks that he is tough and barks out loud.
His small, brown spots look like chocolate drops,
His tail waves like a banner in the air.
When he is showing off he sometimes trots,
When cuddled you are left covered in hair.
He likes to eat everything in sight
And loves to have a quick nap on my bed.
He always pulls and pulls with all his might,
The trick not mastered yet, is playing dead.
However, he always makes me feel glad,
Even when I am feeling very sad!

Alice Blakeley (14)
Northwood College, Northwood

Mr Taylor

Mr Taylor is my English teacher,
In his lessons we are reading plays,
Sometimes I think he should be a preacher,
He is really funny the things he says.

Ev-e-r-y time we mention the word French,
He pretends to spit on the carpet floor,
He reads Shakespeare's plays and acts with hands clenched,
He can be so cool but never a bore.

Mr Taylor always teaches grammar
And makes us understand it really well,
He always writes things down in his planner,
You always get saved by the lesson bell.

When he's bored, he puts his hands on his hips,
Please can you take us on some lovely trips?

Priyanka Kotecha (13)
Northwood College, Northwood

Spring

The seasons have begun, now spring is here.
Crispy leaves crunch, when I put my feet down.
It's sunny, beautiful, nothing to fear!
In the bright sun the leaves turn golden brown,
Pink blossoms fall as I wander about.
The juicy fruits are beginning to grow,
Yellow, dazzling daffodils pop out!
Breezy wind blows and the gleaming stars glow,
Colourful, lively butterflies whizz around,
So much pleasure is spreading everywhere!
The sun is strong, it lifts you off the ground,
It's a sensational breath of fresh air.
The bird is singing sweetly, which is calm,
It sits quietly and gently on my palm.

Falguni Karia (13)
Northwood College, Northwood

A Sonnet About London Zoo

The interesting place called London Zoo,
The home of many amazing creatures.
The chattering birds with feathers of blue,
The penguins too are popular features.

You can feed fish to all the hungry seals,
Or go to the dark room of sleeping bats.
When you see the slithering snakes you'll squeal,
Visit the endangered, roaring, wild cats.

The energetic monkeys should be seen,
The swans swim elegantly on the lake.
The brave can hold lizards with skin of green,
But feeding the giraffes is really great.

So if you would like to be amazed too,
Then be sure that you visit London Zoo.

Rachna Patel (13)
Northwood College, Northwood

Winter

The winter is here, finally it's here,
It's very cold and windy everywhere.
Summer has gone and spring is nowhere near,
It's time to put the heating on and wear

Coats and jumpers, just to make sure you're warm.
It has become very dark from before,
There are very few flowers on my lawn
And now I don't like stepping out the door!

Hats, gloves and scarves are needed now,
Because it is starting to snow as well!
I decide to go out and play, but how?
Just as I decide, I hear the doorbell.

Now, my friends have come to play with me,
Once we played, we went inside to have tea.

Zainab Mustafa (13)
Northwood College, Northwood

The Glistening Rabbit

The rabbit stares and glares at me today,
She looks up at the flower and runs to it,
I wonder if she will come out and play.
I see patchy grass and go and sit,
She looks at me and nibbles at her toes,
Her eyes are sparkling and glistening,
We sit there like a tree and make a pose.
She is so furry and so fluffy too,
I hope the summer will not fade so soon,
I won't see the rabbits if it is cold,
I will need to go in because it's noon.
I wish I could take the rabbit and hold,
But if there is no rabbit outside now,
I wonder if summer will end right now.

Sruti Dupaguntla (12)
Northwood College, Northwood

Forgive Me

This terrible ruin, our world today,
Our desperate war, which can never cease,
Unless we finally have the courage to say,
'I'm sorry, forgive me, let us live in peace.'
If you pray for those who persecute you,
Then God will accept you in His domain.
If you hate them for whatever they do,
The world must live in endless crying pain.
Follow the teachings of a Christian,
Forgive those who did the frightful wrong,
Do not continue hate of tradition
And friendship will grow ever so strong.
Show your love every day that you live
And be sure that you can always forgive.

Lilian Knight (13)
Northwood College, Northwood

The Haunted House

I'm standing here beside the broken door,
The paint is peeling and covered all in dust,
As the dust falls it hits the concrete floor,
The little mouse runs after the bread crust.

The spider crawls out of the dirty drain,
The creaky floorboards are split into two,
As the wind gushes against the windowpane,
The rats are crawling out of the foul loo.

As I walk up the creaky staircase,
My mind wonders as to what is in store,
On the last stair my pulse begins to race,
In front of me I see a shadowed floor.

Beads of sweat dripping down my body,
It's scary. Who'd do this as a hobby?

Sophie Wright (13)
Northwood College, Northwood

The Rock

The rock stands proud, alone yet pleased this day,
Looks down on others, sits on grainy sand.
'I rule you all, my humble slaves I say!
For I'm the largest rock in all the land!'

'We hate this rock that always bullies us,'
Says Stew the stone, the smallest of the lot.
They all agreed, the pebbles had it sussed,
'It's time for action! Let us plan and plot.'

Next day begins, they gather up as one,
They hack and hit, the huge rock is no more.
They celebrate as their job is done,
The rock is left there, sombre, sick and sore.

This proves a valuable little point,
We're strongest when us little ones are joint.

Zara Malik (13)
Northwood College, Northwood

Life To Death

My heart is pounding
I am running
But not sure who from
I have to be strong
Because I know my fears will soon be gone

I am running home
To where I know I am free
Back to the blistering sun
The truthful sands
Away from the harsh torture of a gun

The never-ending stairs of time
Await my steps
On the other side there lies my life
My heart and soul
Never again to be under the threat of a knife

I turn around
To see a man with a rifle
I run as fast as I can
He keeps on gaining and gaining on me
How can I outrun this man?

I see a light at the end of my journey
My fear vanishes
I see hope!
My time has come
I am home

I run to my mother
Relief and ecstasy
I reach out my hand
But I hear a gunshot
Everything goes black.

Anika Parmar (12)
Northwood College, Northwood

My Week

Monday, wake up and take a look outside,
Grotty weather that makes me want to hide.

Tuesday, the sun comes out over the slide,
Get to school and do the drill, what a ride.

Wednesday pupils, teachers by the score,
Lots of things to do and people to see.

Thursday means lots of lessons I adore,
History, English, physics, maths, chemistry.

Friday is the end of the school week,
No more instructions and no more rules.

Saturday, the day for sun all day long,
Going shopping and getting something cool.

Sunday, the day to relax and cool down,
Only to find out that the week goes around.

Jessie Stern (13)
Northwood College, Northwood

The Outsider

He comes on one sunny, sticky morning
He is the new boy, the strange outsider
They all reject him, he does have feelings.
They ignored him, they could have been kinder.
It was an October day when they came.
It started with verbal abuse that day.
The gang surrounded him and said he was lame.
He didn't dare whimper, he started to pray.
He trudged back to his flat, black and blue.
He felt insecure but he stayed very strong.
The gang were in his mind in whatever he did.
He started to break down and got a stitch
And that is the tale of poor secluded Mitch.

Charlotte West (12)
Northwood College, Northwood

Abandoned Identity

As she hides in the desert deep,
Fear and pain awake from their sleep.

From Jigalong to Moore River,
Home and back,
Carrying not a morsel of grub in her sack.

Stolen generation,
From Mr Devil they hide,
Covering their tracks,
The spirit bird will guide.

Hunger fiercely stabs her heart,
Sweltering heat not seconds apart.

Secluded on this hostile plain,
The whites and the tracker,
After her again.

The fiery horizon with gold, orange, red,
The only thing remaining is her, lying dead.

Sonali Shah (12)
Northwood College, Northwood

Deserted Desert Haikus

Intense heat beats down
Walking the dry and cracked earth
Blistering sand stirs

Blazing sun burns us
Deserted dusty plains end
Motionless trees now

The sand goes reddish
Patience for hunger has stopped
Our time has ended.

Sarah Sayeed (12)
Northwood College, Northwood

Angry

Sometimes I feel so angry I could die
I grit my teeth and clench my fist so tight
I stamp about and kick or shout and cry
All I really want is to start a fight
I hate my sister so, so very much
She had to tear my schoolbook, I'm so mad
I slap her face and give her a small punch
Her eyes are red and her face is so sad
A sudden rush of guilt has just arrived
I feel so mean for hitting her so hard
I apologised, well at least I tried
To make her forgive me I send a card
Alas, the devil has forgiven me
But I've to take her on a shopping spree!

Roshni Kanabar (13)
Northwood College, Northwood

My Pink Sonnet

I love to sleep in my warm bed at night
It makes me feel like I am on cloud nine
All dark and black feeling, like I've lost sight
Huddle up, all warm and snug, I'll be fine
I love list'ning to music in the day
Bring up the beat goes boom, boom, shake your thing
The best songs come out in the month of May
Playing xtina makes me wanna sing
All you guys out there, you don't make me smile
I don't need diamond rings or a flash Benz
It's just plain an' simple, you'll run a mile
Can't I do what I want without you getting fenz?
There's things I wanna shout, so let it be
Let's see if you can get by without me.

Rahee Bhagani (13)
Northwood College, Northwood

Racial Prejudice

Native Australians were sent to stay,
Places which were far from their homes, far away.

Because of their skin colour they were abused,
If they tried to run away,
Their hair was cut and skin was bruised.

After all that suffering they were expected to appreciate it,
'It was all for their own good, every bit.'

That's how three sisters were sick to the core
And they couldn't stand it anymore.

Staggering through the blazing heat,
Empty stomachs, aching feet.

Only two managed to get away,
One was caught, forced to stay.

That's how prejudiced some people can be,
It was horrendous, that's plain to see.

What's even worse is that people still
Are racist enough to abuse and kill.

Noor Mansour (12)
Northwood College, Northwood

As You Don't Necessarily Like It

Today our English teacher told us all,
'Go home and write a sonnet if you can.'
I tried, I thought, it drove me up the wall,
That poet Shakespeare, what a clever man!
Syllabic verse is such a pain tonight,
Come on! Come on! I'm running out of time!
And rhythm too, I have to get that right.
But hey, I'm there! I've found the perfect rhyme.
'Twelfth Night' or 'What You Will', 'Othello' too,
'The Comedy Of Errors' and 'Macbeth',
'The Tempest' and 'The Taming Of The Shrew',
These plays have life, his sonnets bore to death.
One line to go, I'm almost there, ti-tum,
As long as you ti-tum, ti-tah, ti-tum!

Philippa Deacon (13)
Northwood College, Northwood

Harvest

Harvest time comes in autumn; crispy and brown
It's a very yellow and golden time
Fields of corn dance in the swishing breeze
Moving and swaying as it is about to be disturbed.

The huge combine harvester's large, turning blades
Slice through the golden corn
As it empties the field.

The fields lie empty as winter arrives
Waiting patiently for snow to fall in silent flakes; cold and frosty
Another year passes by
Now again we wait for harvest time.

Dale Nicholls (12)
Royal National Orthopaedic Hospital School, Stanmore

Back-Breaking Work!

To all the staff on Coxen Ward,
You all deserve a big reward,
For looking after me
And for making me happy!

It was a bit of a scare,
When I was in intensive care,
Outside it may be raining,
But in there it was entertaining!

All the nurses were always busy,
When I first got up, I was very dizzy,
When I got out of bed,
I felt like a heap of lead!

My brace is now ready,
I now need to learn to walk steady,
Even though I had to do with a corset,
And a neighbour that wasn't quite with it!

The nurses always had a smile,
When they were walking up the aisle,
Every hour it was time for the obs,
This caused a few sobs!

I made a little friend,
When I was on the mend,
It was painful when the stitches came out,
But after that I could get round and about!

I have got over the worst,
I felt like I was cursed,
I can't wait to get home,
So I can use the telephone!

I'm really going to miss you so much,
Because you had the very touch,
You all ran up the lane,
When I was in so much pain!

Rhiannon Maylin (12)
Royal National Orthopaedic Hospital School, Stanmore

Harvest

H appy in autumn
A pples fall off the trees
R ipe and ready to eat
V ery juicy and sweet
E very farmer gathers his crops
S ummer has passed
T ime to enjoy the harvest.

Rebecca Moss (13)
Royal National Orthopaedic Hospital School, Stanmore

Deep Within My Heart

Forever together, hand in hand, shoulder to shoulder, side by side,
Someone who can make any place feel like home,
Happiness, laughter and joy filled their soul,
Reflection of their memories in their eyes, bright and beaming,
Kindness, affection and compassion they share,
Care, help, protect and concern, guard,
Friends that will last a lifetime,
Smiles lit up their faces,
Love, cherish, idolise and treasure,
Family, flesh, blood, kin,
I'll build my world and hopes around you,
Everlasting, long gazes,
I see hope in their hearts that these moments will last a lifetime.

Tears burst like ripe fruit,
A flood of remembrance, I weep for the past,
From dawn till dusk remember me.
Their love and affection will always be near,
Deep within my mind I hear your gentle voice whisper my name,
Deep within my heart I can still see you,
Deep within my soul I feel your presence,
Deep within me you are still here.
I'll be there forever until the end,
I am your best friend.

Lauren Jones (12)
St Catherine's School, Twickenham

In The Mind Of The Child

Nutcase
Head case
Staring into space
In space
Trying to place
Where the dark things live.

Darkness occurs
Rapidly occurring
Through the seams of existence
Where the dark things live.

In the cinema with pictures
Clashing
Thrashing
In the mind of the child
Where the dark things live.

Angelic faces though
Sweet and childish
Are hiding the power
That they hold
In the mind of a child
Where the dark things live.

But when you've grown older
And you die in the mind
You forget where
The dark things live
In the mind of the child

Where the dark things live . . .

Laura Greenwood (13)
St Catherine's School, Twickenham

The Show

Intense, bedazzling, eye-catchingly amazing,
For one night only the show comes alive.
Hours of practise all for this one moment,
Capture it forever, frozen in time.
Concentration on their faces, determination in their hearts,
Words of the choreographer in their heads.
Anticipation from the audience, admiration from the fans

This is it. The night you'll always remember. This is it!

The curtains open,
The lights dim down.
There is silence from the crowd,
The dance begins.

The intense, bedazzling, eye-catchingly amazing dance
Instantly hypnotizes the audience,
In awe of the synchronized movements of their bodies.

They dance for their lives,
They dance like it's the last.
They dance for everything they have achieved.

The dance ends. The music stops.
The dancers freeze instantaneously.
But in their hearts they are dancing,
In their souls they are alive.
For they have done it.

The dancers bow,
The curtain falls.
Applause fills the room.

That was it. The night you'll never forget. That was it!

Aurien Joseph (12)
St Catherine's School, Twickenham

My Dog

He's loveable
I admire him
I adore him and treasure him
I love him.
I have concern for him
Keep him
Cherish and guard him
I care for him.
He makes me smile
I feel happy when I'm with him
I feel cheerful and I fill with delight
When he greets me at the door.
He makes me happy when I am down
I need him.
He's mine
To care for
To look after
And my own to love
I am responsible for him.
All these things,
Love, care, need and responsibility
Mean one thing:
He's my dog!

Rosie O'Callaghan (12)
St Catherine's School, Twickenham

Who Are You To Me?

When you and I are together,
We can face the world.
You carry me when I am weak,
You never let me fall.

You and I can lift a weight,
That we couldn't do alone.
You make me want to dance,
You make me want to laugh.

We are forever in unison,
Nothing's stopping us.
We can go on forever,
Holding on together.

Whenever I need you,
You're there with your words,
Giving me help,
When I need you the most.

Things that are impossible to me,
You are able to do.
Things I'm going to do,
You're there before me.

Without you I'd be at a loss,
A bird without its wings,
A book without its cover,
A park without its tree,

A body without a soul.

Taneesha Gadher (12)
St Catherine's School, Twickenham

Never Falling Out

My family is a fruit bowl,
Always bumping into each other.
There to help when I ripen up,
Picking up pieces as I roll around.
The bowl is eventually getting smaller and smaller,
As we grow bigger and bigger,
We now have to work even harder together.
Making sure we do not fall off the edge,
By being careful and aware.
Mistakes happen, that's how I learn,
But I now know that forever and ever,
They will be there for me.
Making sure I fall into their hands
And together I will follow them,
Out of the bowl,
For a journey that will not end.

Divya Vatish (12)
St Catherine's School, Twickenham

Bored

Sitting on a shelf day and night
Getting weaker
Watching people walking in
Brushing their hair
With a grimy hairbrush
Worth nothing, just a stick-like bottle
Bored stiff.
Shampoo liquid rushing up and down
My plastic side
Like a book
No life in me
Standing there
Until the last drop's gone . . .

Christina Braitchouk (11)
St Catherine's School, Twickenham

Free

Tranquil, serene sea inspires
Open, endless waters entice
Peaceful, delicate waves move slenderly
Free, concise splashes enter the air

The vivid dreams of nature are no longer dreams
Dolphins effortlessly leap with grace
Majestic, dignified creatures show their true colours
Elegance takes over the ocean.

Rhiannon Nagra (13)
St Catherine's School, Twickenham

Usher

Personality, a bit of a mysterious guy
Cheeky, likes to have a play around
Eye-catcher, he has an eye for the ladies
Bad boy, also known as the troublemaker
Adventurous, a daring daredevil
Stylish, but sophisticated
Model, but also a show-off
Dancer, he was made for the dance floor
Singer, with an attitude.

Rhondda Ramdin (13)
St Catherine's School, Twickenham

English

E nglish is great,
N ever gets boring,
G irls and boys enjoy it,
L ovely to learn,
I t is always fun,
S tories are cool,
H owever, you will always enjoy English.

Emma-Louise Peachey (12)
Sunbury Manor School, Sunbury-upon-Thames

Paradise

The colour of the grass
So green and lush
The soft, red sky
Like an innocent blush.
And the rustle of leaves
On the tall oak trees
And the coolness and calm
Of a day's dusk breeze.
The trickle of a stream
So gentle and slow
And the silhouettes of fish
And their slight orange glow.
Is this called Paradise
Or is it just me?
Is this the place
We all want to be?

Sam Wisden (14)
Sunbury Manor School, Sunbury-upon-Thames

Rocky - The Last Straw

People want to see you fight
But it's in the middle of the night.
Someone goes to dodge a kick
But your moves are too slick.
You get rewarded some day
But Mr T says you'll pay.
You say you're scared in the ring
Until you hear the loud ding.
It's round one and you're knocked out
Now your trainers are giving the shout.
The fight is over and you lost
Now you know Mr T is the boss.

Harry West (12)
Sunbury Manor School, Sunbury-upon-Thames

EastEnders Ballad

EastEnders is a popular TV show,
With the Slaters - Charlie, Kat and Mo.
There's also Lynn, who's married to Gary
And scheming Janine, who killed Barry.

Alfie marrying Kat was quite handy,
For she was once engaged to Andy.
Spencer really fancies Zoe,
Sonia had a daughter who she named Chloe.

Tariq knew he was a brother,
But the Feirraras never knew there was another.
They nearly lost their house because of their dad,
Because of him, money troubles were bad.

Janine held a grudge against Laura,
Never had any sympathy for her,
So when Laura mysteriously died,
Janine was in trouble when the police arrived.

Vicki had a test to see if love was in the air,
It turned out Spencer and Kelly made a perfect pair.
Zoe and Dennis were not meant to be,
But this, Zoe really could not see.

When Martin Fowler's brother died,
Sonia was there, by his side.
He then realised they were meant to be
And wrote in candles, 'Marry me'.

There is always trouble in Albert Square,
Some things that happen aren't really fair.
EastEnders won the award for the 'Best British Soap',
They'll win it again next year, we hope!

April McCoig (13)
Sunbury Manor School, Sunbury-upon-Thames

The Ballad Of The Russian Siege

There was a Russian siege,
At least two hundred died,
It was a three-day crisis,
Many of them cried.

Excited children went to school,
To see all of their friends,
They never knew they'd never see home,
Or that their life might even end.

They trapped them in the gym,
It was really, really crammed,
The terrorists were proud,
The door was also slammed.

The siege was on a Wednesday morning,
All were hot and tired,
The terrorists were really mean
And all the guns were fired.

There were thirty hostage-takers,
It ended Saturday evening,
They stripped to their underwear,
Many of them stopped breathing.

Violence began as medical workers,
Drove to the school,
To collect injured and dead bodies,
To go straight to the hall.

Ninety-two people were in critical condition,
The day's events took Moscow by surprise,
It was another grim reminder of terrorism,
The mystery why still lies.

Zoe Harrison (12)
Sunbury Manor School, Sunbury-upon-Thames

The Holocaust

Why were people shot and killed,
Thrown in gas chambers, door then sealed?
Why were people filled with pain?
What did Hitler think he'd gain?

Children robbed of their toys,
Men separated, starving boys,
Young and dying boys and girls,
Women stripped of their curls.

Why did this ever occur?
Pain or peace, would you prefer?
This cruelty then had rocked the world,
Six million Jews, their minds were whirled!

Before they died, their bodies were stripped,
The hatred so extravagant, like being whipped.
Jaws cut out,
There was no doubt.

Why did the Germans act so intent?
People starved to such an extent,
Chucked into heaps like lumps of lard,
The surviving Jews were mentally scarred.

Close families kept apart,
Life after death . . . the only good start.
This tragic holocaust never forgot,
So many Jews, the Germans wiped the lot!

Georgia Brown (13)
Sunbury Manor School, Sunbury-upon-Thames

Shopping

Shopping is cool,
I love it all.
Getting the bus,
There's loads of fuss.
Pay my fare,
We're nearly there.
Bus has stopped,
Let's begin to shop.
Buying special things,
Like gold rings.
Flowers and all,
They look really cool.
Lots of noise,
Babies with their toys.
In McD,
Who can I see?
I'll take a seat,
So I can eat.
Got a skirt,
Now I can flirt.
Waiting at the till,
To pay my bill.
Most of my money's gone,
Time to move on.
Found a great top,
Now it's time to stop.

Claire Dillistone (12)
Sunbury Manor School, Sunbury-upon-Thames

The Holocaust!

I dream about you nearly every night
The pain, the anger and the fright.
It's hard to imagine how they got through
With all that was done to them, by you.
Every waking hour you made them regret,
You decided that you would not let them forget,
That what they believed in wasn't true
And the ones who were right, were you.
You cut off the women's curls
And took away their precious pearls,
You even had the children's toys,
From all the mothers you took their girls and boys.
You dumped their bodies, left for rotten,
But there is something that will never be forgotten,
The pain that was caused,
By you, the holocaust.

Juliette Birt (13)
Sunbury Manor School, Sunbury-upon-Thames

The Holocaust

The holocaust lasted for twelve years,
It caused so much sadness and fear.
Peace, happiness and joy,
Were taken from every girl and boy.
Replaced by suffering, fear and fright,
Watching while people were killed day and night.
All they could do was sit and cry,
While they saw their parents die.
So many of them lost their lives,
Some were lucky to survive.
Six million Jews suffered in pain,
What did Hitler think he'd gain?
Thinking about it brings a tear to the eye,
Why did it happen? Why?

Daniel Walsh (13)
Sunbury Manor School, Sunbury-upon-Thames

The Ballad Of A Tornado

The tornado hit and the building fell,
Suzanne said that it was hell,
Desks, tables, chairs and doors,
Fell drastically to the floors.

The seven people in the building,
Scared to death and had bad feelings,
No one died, a few hurt,
Except the poor man, Mr Burt.

This happened at 5.30,
People were jumpy and dirty,
Families waiting, waiting, waiting,
For their parents who were shaking.

The beast was going at a speed,
The building was flattened like a weed,
It carried on for six more miles,
Then the tornado stopped for a while.

'It was vicious and scary,'
Said a secretary named Mary,
She survived and was glad,
So were her mum and dad.

Now it was over, but people could never forget,
The drastic thing that happened to them!

Samantha Roberts (12)
Sunbury Manor School, Sunbury-upon-Thames

When The Three Lions Roar

The beautiful passion
The three lions roar
We can do it
Just like before.

Passing, shooting
Tackling, scoring
Running, roaring
England soaring.

Singing, cheering
For our pride
Playing together
Side by side.

The second millennium
Didn't matter
Now we're stronger
Than ever.

We came nearer in 1990
We rose in '66
We can do it
With our skilful tricks.

Come on England
We'll see
What you can do
Over the English sea.

Josh Standing (12)
Sunbury Manor School, Sunbury-upon-Thames

The Prison Bell

The convicted goes to his prison cell,
Waiting for the prison bell;
Thinks of escape routes in his dreams,
Makes up many elaborate schemes.

Goes to the dining hall,
Has great fun, what a ball;
Food fights really are great,
Even throw knives, forks and plates.

Tries to wash in the shower,
Tries to drown, now or never;
Now he is dead, we've got a free bed,
For another criminal to cower.

Now the process begins again,
The new inmate is called Ben;
A serial murderer, they say,
Better warn the others away.

Johnathan Bridger (13)
Sunbury Manor School, Sunbury-upon-Thames

The Ballad Of Hillsborough

H illsborough was the biggest disaster
I n football that I know,
L iverpool was where it happened,
L ive on a TV show.
S o many people crushed,
B etween the struggling fans,
O n a day that should have been happy,
R ejoiced by every man.
O ver ninety died and
U nder the rushing bodies on the ground they lie,
G irls and boys and men and women,
H ow they let it happen, I really wonder why?

Jack Haslett (12)
Sunbury Manor School, Sunbury-upon-Thames

The Russian Siege

Excited children came to school
To see their new friends
They never realised they'd never go home
Or that their lives might end.

Some of them were young
Some of them were old
There were a lot of terrorists
Their blood was freezing cold.

They took them to the gym
They all stood around
Everyone was really squashed
The terrorists were proud.

It started Wednesday morning
It ended Saturday evening
Everyone was hot and tired
Some of them stopped breathing.

Gunfire and explosions
Erupted Friday morning
Two hundred of them killed
The end day of its drawing.

A little boy cried
His mother and sister gone
The terrorists were smiling
They really thought they'd won.

The hostages panicked
Some tried to flee
It was hot and smoky
Some couldn't see.

It was horrible to see
So many children ill
Everyone was very upset
The noise was like a drill.

Jade Bristow (12)
Sunbury Manor School, Sunbury-upon-Thames

Titanic

They waved goodbye to their friends
As they boarded the ship, Titanic
They left the dock in tears
But they didn't know it would end in a panic.

Everyone dressed up
The luxury liner so comfortable and posh
All the things you need
And lots of people with lots of dosh.

Days and days passed
The fun had almost come to the end
They had almost reached New York
They had all made so many friends.

They soon felt a bang
A huge iceberg the liner had hit
Everyone was shocked
Many people were having fits.

On the date of the 15th
At 2.20am the ship had split
Everyone was screaming
They were all so shocked about the hit.

The ship went down and down
About 1,500 lives were lost
Famous people died
The ship went down with a lot of cost.

Years and years passed
1985 soon came
The wreck of the Titanic was found
It was such a shame.

The Titanic was found in two pieces
JP Morgan owned it
The ship had many pieces
EJ Smith was the captain of the ship.

Amy Jopson (12)
Sunbury Manor School, Sunbury-upon-Thames

The Dunblane Massacre

As I cleaned my cupboard,
A news report I found,
Made me shocked and angry,
Made me want to frown.

Amazing that just one school,
Could be ruined by such a nutter,
With sixteen now dead,
No single word can they utter.

Thomas Hamilton was his name,
A madman I should think,
To do such a terrible act,
He must've been on the brink!

Even the Queen was outraged,
The Prime Minister at Downing Street too,
All I can say is,
You're lucky it wasn't you!

For we can stand and pray for them all,
But we don't know what it feels like
To go through
Such horror, such pain, such fright!

Megan Dunsby (12)
Sunbury Manor School, Sunbury-upon-Thames

The Snowman

As I stand on the frozen ground,
I watch all the snowflakes float all around.
As soft as a cushion, as white as a ghost,
Winter is the season that I like the most.

Rebecca Harris (11)
Sunbury Manor School, Sunbury-upon-Thames

Best Things

Orange juice with my lovely dinner,
Hooray! I am the poetry competition winner,
My dad whistling his favourite tunes,
Saturday morning watching cartoons.

Mr Achmed teaching us to add,
Someone being very, very bad,
The taste of sweet chocolate cakes,
The view of crystal clear lakes.

In art we are making colourful tones,
My sister, Sally, won't leave me alone,
Sunny Spain, we are going tomorrow,
My friend's wicked sunglasses I borrow.

Today my pocket money,
Winnie the Pooh eating honey,
I love drinks that are fizzy,
Spinning around makes me dizzy.

Emma, who is insane,
Sitting on the windowpane,
Writing and drawing,
Getting up late in the morning.

Mum coming to say goodnight,
I have a nightmare, what a fright,
Thorpe Park is so much fun,
When the day is nearly done.

Going clothes shopping,
With all the bags I am nearly dropping,
Fluffy cats,
Tombola hats.

Red, yellow, pink and blue,
One plus one equals two,
Doing my homework all day,
I have nothing else to say!

Helen Curry (12)
Sunbury Manor School, Sunbury-upon-Thames

Darkness

Such a joy to feel free wind blowing through my hair,
No longer held in transfixing stare.
I ran through the forest; no need to look back,
The moon was bright, the darkness black.
And I ran on and onwards, a joy to be free,
As I ran I felt the touch of every tree.
I decided to rest, free in my heart,
I picked fruit from the trees, the flavour was tart.
So as I lay down, the darkness embraced me,
I did not jump or start but embraced it freely.
And as I lay down and fell asleep,
I was so very happy, I started to weep.
And asleep there on the bracken I lay,
The darkness enveloped me, perpetual and grey.

Andrew Voneshen (12)
Sunbury Manor School, Sunbury-upon-Thames

At The Farm

Pink pigs, cute, cuddly, small, fat
Just like that.
Sandy dog, old and bold, not very playful
But good as gold.
Chicks chirp around, chirping till they
Fall to the ground.
Playful ponies, pretty and polite, playing all day
Till it's not that light.
Dancing ducks, waddling alone, till they bump into you,
'Oh, hello!'
Shy sheep, curly and cute, being sheared,
Oh! what a sight.

Paige Fitzsimmons (11)
Sunbury Manor School, Sunbury-upon-Thames

Hate And Conflict

Hate is in the air, I wouldn't want to share it!
Not even old Mrs McConkey could bear it!
So they would have had to make a dare,
Or it would have come up in a flare!
But there was still someone to blame,
Tommy, Sadie, they're all the same,
Protestants, don't put them to shame.

No one likes Belfast,
Even that boy Kevin, the one with the cast,
It was a blast, but it still went too fast!
What, what, it's always been hot,
Watch out for Brian Rafferty, you could get shot.
That boy with the gun, no one would trust him,
Not even his friends sitting right next to him.
Now he is dead and so he is all out of our heads!

Why, oh why, has this world been brought to conflict?
Not even the little old lady could help it.
People have died, people have cried,
No one knows how much it shows,
Even by the way you wear your clothes!

Emma Wall (13)
Sunbury Manor School, Sunbury-upon-Thames

Holocaust

H atred for the Jews
O rganisers of mass murder
L ives taken so violently
O ver one man's sick mind
C hildren's toys lie motionless
A strewn amongst the young
U nrelenting torture
S uffering and pain
T ortured souls in Heaven now rest.

Rebecca Jopson (14)
Sunbury Manor School, Sunbury-upon-Thames

School Siege

He sat and wanted to lie,
As he watched his friends die.
He didn't like it in his school hall,
Waiting for the ceiling to fall.

The rebels blew themselves up,
All the people wanted was water in a cup.
Bombs hanging from floors and ceilings,
All the people had bad feelings.

I was trying to go through the wall,
As more ceiling was going to fall.
Poor little Ahmed came out alive
And wasn't the only one to survive.

Devastated dads and mums,
Waited for their daughters and sons.
Dads and mums wanted it to be a lie,
But daughters and sons had to die.

Over 300 dead,
It will still be in their head.
Many people were hit,
But hopefully the children will get over it.

Hannah Lee (12)
Sunbury Manor School, Sunbury-upon-Thames

A Shakespearean Sonnet

My school day starts when the clock strikes seven,
I toss and turn, but I have to get up.
I jump out of bed, sleepy and leaden
And when I see my friends, I am all 'sup'.
So, when I walk through the blackened school gates,
I hear shouts of, 'You, boy, tuck your shirt in,'
And across the playground I see my mates.
The school bells rings and the lessons begin.
In the lessons we learn many new things;
By lunchtime, my brain is ready to blow.
Football releases the tension it brings,
But it is quite hard to play in the snow.
But anyway, after all, I can say,
I'm so happy at the end of the day.

Conor Moss (13)
Teddington School, Teddington

A Shakespearean Sonnet

I strode down a country lane to the park,
The air was fresh and the sky was so blue,
When from nowhere came my friend, Daniel Clark,
He turned around and said, 'I'll stroll with you.'
We went to a café and ate some food,
A hot cross bun and a chocolate bar.
That put Daniel in a very good mood,
Then we drove off in my little red car.
We drove to the zoo, oh what a big laugh
And saw some penguins and a scary shark.
We should have left, but I saw a giraffe,
Then we had to go, it was getting dark.
Oh golly gosh, Daniel got in a fight,
I took Daniel home and called out, 'Goodnight.'

Rachel O'Hara (13)
Teddington School, Teddington

A Shakespearean Sonnet

Fear

It stalks in every person's mind I know,
It envelops their dreams and their nightmares.
It makes the highest people become low,
It approaches fast when courage is bared.
It stops people from doing what they want,
It prevents them from being really free.
It never goes, just flows like a great font,
It blinds people to what they want to see.
It is portrayed in many different ways,
It is embodied in TV and books,
It is in someone different every day,
You see it when they speak and how they look.
Fear is forever, it can have no doubt,
Once you're pulled in, you can never get out.

Hannah Downer (13)
Teddington School, Teddington

Writing Poems Is Something That Is Hard

Writing poems is something that is hard
Finding a subject takes me a lot of time,
Shakespeare found it easy, he was a bard
For me the biggest problem is to rhyme.
After a while it all can start to work,
Think of a topic, write it in my book.
I fall asleep, then wake up with a jerk
It's not quite right, I'll take another look.
Love poem? What's my opinion of it?
I'm far too young to write about romance
And although love is ideal for a sonnet,
At thirteen I'd be taking quite a chance.
So I'll do what makes me most excited,
Dreaming of a win for Leeds United.

Alexander Hetherington (14)
Teddington School, Teddington

Strange

Round and round I'm spinning,
In and out of space,
Laughter steals my body
And smiles steal my face.
You hacked through my defences,
You tore away my shield,
I just can't help grinning,
'Cause this feeling is so real.
They all say that you're a weirdo,
I can tell you're slightly crazed,
But your words are making magic,
I am dizzy, I am dazed.
Can it ever happen?
Will it ever be?
I hold my breath in waiting
For us two, you and me.

Tallulah Francis (12)
Teddington School, Teddington

A Shakespearean Sonnet

Nature: monkeys swing through rustling trees,
Snakes slither through the intertwining vines,
Flowers chased by bright butterflies and bees,
Frogs become camouflaged, tricking our minds.
Nature: cheetahs are pouncing on their prey,
The roar of the lion echoes throughout,
Whilst all of the baby cubs fight and play,
In water, dolphins jump and play about.
Nature: eagles swoop low and glide so high
The victims, small mammals, scuttle away,
Owls silently fly through the deep blue sky,
Crocodiles lurk beneath the water's bay.
Nature: seals shuffle 'long the sandy beach,
Sharks' streamlined bodies and menacing teeth.

Roxanne Bates (13)
Teddington School, Teddington

A Shakespearean Sonnet

So many children die every day,
In Africa and other poor places.
They work all the time and get little pay.
Some make trainers which also need laces.
They work so many hours every week;
Many don't have food or shelter at home.
Prospects for a future are very bleak;
Slave-drivers don't care, but we'll sure show 'em.
Their mothers and fathers send them away:
They want them to work, to earn decent food.
None of the children have a proper say;
The behaviour of men, at best is rude.
Give a thought about the children in need;
This is not an order, it's just a plead.

Sarah Gowers (13)
Teddington School, Teddington

A Shakespearean Sonnet

The day of the week that I like the best,
Could it be Monday? Could it be Tuesday?
Of course it's Saturday, forget the rest.
Come on, don't you agree with what I say?
No alarm to disturb my happy dreams,
Covers tight around me so I keep warm,
Curtains tightly drawn to keep out sunbeams,
Keep away morning and go away dawn.
Bacon frying, crisp toast, golden and brown,
The romance of a breakfast fills my head,
Too good to ignore, my feet hit the floor,
'You can't have some yet,' my dear mother said.
'Wake up first and wash your sleepy face, son,
You'll get all this good food when you are done.'

James Hindley (13)
Teddington School, Teddington

A Shakespearean Sonnet

This is our play: 'A Midsummer Night's Dream',
The theatre open, the curtains drawn.
But, my friend, at the start this did not seem
Just as smooth and light as a well cut lawn.
You see, to start we did not know our lines
And some weren't prepared to be seen on stage.
The rehearsals were full of moans and whines;
I thought this might take us more than an age.
But slow and steady we managed our parts;
We mustered our strength and conquered our fears.
We were as joyous as hot-headed sparks,
Gladly we saw no more of swelling tears.
So on this night, my friend, be sure to see
The best play of time there can hope to be.

Joss Foster (14)
Teddington School, Teddington

A Shakespearean Sonnet

Your love shields me like great wings from above,
From fear and hatred, thunder, sun and rain;
You bring divine peace, like the turtle dove,
But also crimson and furious pain.
Cupid's sting, just like the thorn of a rose,
Tears out my heart and finds a companion.
Orange blossom sweetness reaches my nose;
My true love's loss is deep as a canyon.
Your velvety skin, so silky and fine
Glows with awesome beauty in the moonlight;
Your hair, with shine that is simply divine,
Makes your eyes shine like diamonds, ever bright.
Beautiful love, bold, brave, silent and strong,
Will last forever, eternally long.

Arthur Mollett (13)
Teddington School, Teddington

Kennings

A headless rider
A wall climber

A sheet scarer
A feet bearer

A knight walker
A medium talker

An item mover
A carpet groover

A moon runner
A doom comer

I'm a . . .

Sam Green (12)
The Cedars School (Pupil Referral Unit), Maidstone

The Dragon

Out of its lair the dragon crashes
Thrashing and rearing the dark stormy skies.
Dragon's breath hot and steamy
Roaring loud and scary
Angry tail waving and wapping
Gigantic claws big and sharp
Orange flames from its jaws burn and smoke
Nails scratch and cut
And the dragon sees its prey
It bursts down to the ground to eat it.

Connor Dawkins (12)
The Cedars School (Pupil Referral Unit), Maidstone

Harvey

H arvey at home
A mazingly tiny
R eally cuddly
V isitors queuing at the door
E xtra skin that's all wrinkly
Y ellow Babygro

S leeps in his cot
I love him very much
M ummy and Daddy are very proud
O nly three weeks old
N appies are small

S ick on Mummy and Daddy
C rying when he's hungry
O ne hundred percent love
T oothless at the moment
T oo cute to be true.

Matthew Scott (12)
The Cedars School (Pupil Referral Unit), Maidstone

Soldier Kennings

A bomb blaster
A cleaning master
A uniform wearer
A trench sharer
A guard at barrier
A rifle carrier
A dead collector
An ammo passer
A warning shouter
A doctor helper
A gun cleaner
A trench digger.

Stuart Hawkins (14)
The Cedars School (Pupil Referral Unit), Maidstone

Romance

Parliament think they're right
Little kids think they're out of sight
Spoilt snobs
I hate that stuff.

Gerrard scoring hat-tricks
Liverpool players pull the chicks
Football
I like that stuff.

Homework, get too much of it
Moaning teachers, I am sick of it
School
I hate that stuff.

The Simpsons is the best cartoon
It has an amazing catchy tune
TV
I like that stuff.

French snails float in it
Vampires die from it
Garlic
I hate that stuff.

Motor cross full of dirt
Super cross you can get hurt
Motorbikes
I like that stuff.

Love hearts, chocolates, sending roses
It annoys me how the boyfriend poses
Romance
I hate that stuff.

Josh Thomas (12)
The Cedars School (Pupil Referral Unit), Maidstone

Kennings

A sofa scratcher
A door basher
A straw eater
A light sleeper
A painful biter
A vicious fighter
A food nicker
A biscuit nibbler
A cracker grabber
A nose twitcher
She's my . . .

Tara Fraser (13)
The Cedars School (Pupil Referral Unit), Maidstone

Family

Family is always there for you,
No matter what the things you do.
With families you always have lots of fun,
Playing with your brothers in the sun.

Parents are mostly playful with you,
Unless they have work to do.
When your parents cannot play,
Your brothers or sisters come right away.

Family can be pulled away from you,
Sometimes there's nothing you can do.
Even if they're taken away,
There's nothing you can do or say.

You must seem kind and if you do,
You will never regret if they go too.
Because you don't know when they will go,
When they leave you must go with the flow.

Pierce Dargan (11)
The Harrodian School, Barnes

Stars

Stars are so very beautifully bright
They're so gorgeous,
When I lie down
And watch them twinkling in the night.

Stars are like diamonds
Sparkling away,
Worth much more than one trillion pounds
Which no one can ever pay.

Stars are so tremendously far away
That at night on the beach,
The sea can only take a glimpse
Of stars that can never be reached.

Stars are so gorgeous at night I say
And then along comes the day and takes the twinkles away,
I love stars, they are so pretty
And if we lost such marvellous things, it would be oh, such a pity.

Lara Knight (11)
The Harrodian School, Barnes

Egypt

Egypt, Egypt, glorious Egypt
Hot, boiling and sweltering Egypt
But beware, follow the mirage and you'll meet your doom
Where sandstorms and suffocating heat will loom.

Tombs, tombs, frightening tombs
Wind through passages and find the tomb
But beware, you'll meet your doom
If you stay near the shadows where mummified bodies loom.

The Nile, the Nile, the expansive Nile
Where crocodiles and other creatures vile
Will lurk in the shining waters and wait
For beware, swim in its waters and before long, you're the bait!

James Hickmann (11)
The Harrodian School, Barnes

My Life

I am sitting in a damp corner
Nothing to play with
No one to be with.
My arms are turning different colours
My hair feels like it's coming out.
How I wish for a better life
Arms to hug me, a caring family
People to love me.
But these dreams I know will never come true.
At school no one talks to me
No one plays with me.
I hear footsteps, these are the bringers of pain.
An arm lashes out, a hand strikes me
I fall to the hard wood floor.
I've been sent to my room
I'm getting skinnier by the day
Nobody knows
Nobody cares
Maybe I'm just dreaming
A terrible nightmare.

Patrick Synnott (11)
The Harrodian School, Barnes

Seaside

The seaside is a wonderful place to be
When I swim the fishes circle around me.

All kind of colours for the eye to see
The sea is the best place to be.

Beaches are the nicest place to see
But the best beach of all is in Italy.

The sea is warm when the sun shines on it
But nothing goes better with the sea than family!

Max Cantellow (11)
The Harrodian School, Barnes

What To Do A Poem On?

What to do a poem on?
So many things to choose from.
Maybe pirates collecting gold,
Or riding upon a penny fathom.

The leopard stalking the antelope,
A squirrel in a tree,
So many things to put in my poem but,
To be or not to be?

Scuba diving underwater,
An angel playing a harp,
What to choose, which to pick,
Goldfish, piranha, carp?

The animal world sounds interesting,
With the lion king of what will walk,
Up in the sky is a whole new world,
With the leader as the mighty hawk.

But then you think about people,
Civilization at its best,
The latest electronics,
Beat all the rest.

There's still the problem of picking subject,
All these marvellous things,
The animals, the people,
The queens and all the kings.

So I think I'd better get started,
This is going to be fun,
Oh no, now I have a problem,
My poem's already done.

Claire Wegener (11)
The Harrodian School, Barnes

Tigers

Sleek, dark, pitch-black stripes
Bright orange like fruit, soft and ripe
He creeps through the bush
No noise at all, *shush!*

Chasing prey, ready for a meal
He waits, sitting or kneeling
Legs bent, ready to pounce
1, 2, 3 he counts.

Ready to take the neck
Sees a bug, an almost invisible speck
The animal prepares for lunch
Antelope by the bunch!

This is his life
And maybe even a tiger wife
Eating raw food
A tiger and his deadly brood.

Nick Aston (11)
The Harrodian School, Barnes

New York City

N oisy streets at night
E xhaust floating about
W ater polluted in the channel

Y ankees beat the Red Sox
O rdinary trains pull into Central Station
R ough gangs mug people
K ing of all cities

C olliding people on a crowded sidewalk
I ncredible saves at the ice hockey rink
T all buildings scraping the sky
Y ankees win the World Series.

Buck Goggin (11)
The Harrodian School, Barnes

Why?

Why does the rain fall from the sky?
Why do birds have wings to fly?

Why do ballerinas stand on their toes?
Why do little girls wear pretty pink clothes?

Why do flowers bloom in the spring?
Why do married people have to wear a ring?

Why does the snow fall so white?
Why does the moon shine so bright?

Why do rivers never stop flowing?
Why do stars never stop glowing?

Why do the French love to eat snail?
Why does a happy dog wag its tail?

Why has God made all these things?
Let's be thankful for all that God brings.

Tania Faik (11)
The Harrodian School, Barnes

Hallowe'en

H allowe'en is exciting
    When you hear the monsters scream in the night
A nd as the clock strikes midnight,
    The country's full of fright.
L ots of spirits come out to play,
    Ready to put up a fight,
L eft, right, left, right, tragic is their plight.
O ouuhh, howl the werewolves,
    As they uncurl from a ball,
W hile helpless children scream
    And run to find shelter in the hall.
E njoying their feast, the werewolves
E at the children with their shoes and shirts.
N ever before has Hallowe'en provided such delicious desserts.

Melinda Remme (11)
The Harrodian School, Barnes

In My Dark And Smelly Fridge!

I find milk, that has gone very sour,
Turning into cheese, hour by hour.

I find a key from a pirate's treasure chest,
And mouldy eggs from a vulture's nest.

I find butter, like cream it is,
And several old Cokes that have lost their fizz.

I find a slice of cake from my parents' anniversary,
This was way back, when I was at nursery!

Finally I found what I was looking for,
Underneath an old apple core.

I take out and eat a packet of crisps,
All of that, for only this!

Francesca Levi Morenos (12)
The Harrodian School, Barnes

The Snowy Woods

Dripping snowdrops from the shadowed trees,
Dawn is near for the wintered creatures of those who glee,
The snow will not melt until 8 o'clock this evening,
For the sunshine is sizzling.

The footprints of the fox, deer and even sometimes bear,
Will pass over while the snow still covers,
Taking every inch of dust,
Time goes on and it gets cooler and darker,
For those who are deadly at nightfall.

The fox, deer and bear prints have now faded from the sun,
Nothing to see, now it has all gone,
Only the deadly creatures can see and hear at nightfall,
Until morning they will feast.

Rowena Kealey (12)
The Harrodian School, Barnes

Polar Bear

In a dusty corner
Of an old museum
A mother is waiting for her child

Moth-eaten fur coat
Arctic-blue eyes
And the trace of what could be a smile

Nose pressed against the glass
She watches them play

She once had one of her own
But it would have long passed away

They stare, they stare
With eyes of life

Never a softer pair has she seen
Than the one in white
With pink shoes.

Georgina King (11)
The Harrodian School, Barnes

The Cry Of Mino

The pain ricocheted around my mind,
Sending anger pulsing through my body.
I shouldn't have let you stay so far behind,
My lush, quiet Mino.

I should have heard your flames cry out to me,
Oh, how I miss your mountains and the birds.
I remember my dear, beloved family,
And that cry I want to demolish from my mind.

That iron, ghostly figure of death,
Sliding his blade in your people's flesh.
You now do not even hear one person's breath,
For you are nothing, only your cry lives on.

Nils Astrand (11)
The Harrodian School, Barnes

Autumn

The leaves fall off the trees, golden, ruby and yellow,
All crisp and mellow.
The cold air bites your toes and freezes your nose!
Swish is the sound of the leaves being blown around,
Crunch is the sound of feet treading over the wet leaves
On the ground.
Children are running about who yell and shout.
They are going bonkers about conkers.
Glowing and shining bright, the conkers pop out of their spiky cases
And they all have clean, brown faces.

As darkness falls, Hallowe'en has arrived.
The children all get ready and have a big surprise!
A feast of delicious treats that all the children will eat.
As the door shuts,
The voices of many other children are all calling,
'Trick or treat,' that echoes around the streets.

Saffron Rizzo (11)
The Harrodian School, Barnes

Winter

When the first snow falls
And the land is suffocated,
In a blanket of whiteness.

When the first snowballs are thrown
And snowmen are made,
By happy children in the powerful winds.

When the little robin redbreast
Chirps on the frosty fence,
Hoping for a morsel of food.

And when your children and yourselves
Sit all cosy and warm,
Toasting, in front of a roaring fire.

Bryony Harrower (11)
The Harrodian School, Barnes

Night

As I gaze up into the black night sky,
I see the clouds slowly pass by,
The moonlight is so pure and white,
I watch those glazing stars at night.

I see the stars shine so bright,
Giving out their silver light,
I watch the night that never does die,
I hear the sound of ocean waves nearby.

The lights of the aeroplane are so bright,
As it makes its final flight,
Scientists try with all their might,
To reach the planets placed at such a great height.

The seagulls do cry as over mountains they fly,
The wind howls and soars around,
The black curtain does surround all trees and nature to be found
And I sit and listen to this amazing sound.

I feel I can reach out and touch the night,
Oh, what a beautiful sight.

Farah Kassam (14)
The Harrodian School, Barnes

Monkeys

M any different monkeys,
O rang-utan and chimpanzee,
N ot every monkey is brown, they are all different colours
   and unique,
K ind and mean ones,
E vil ones, they all have one thing in common,
   they swing from branch to branch,
Y ellow bananas are what they eat,
S limy, yummy and soft.

Lettie Coad (11)
The Harrodian School, Barnes

The Tube Station

Silent people press into the dim light and their destination.
Echoes of footsteps of the other mortals,
Sound around the circular walls.
The tube departs and shoots down the tunnel,
Like a bullet down a gun.
People rock back and forth reading their newspapers,
Trying to be oblivious to the juveniles' music
Blaring out of their headphones.
Then the doors slide open and more commuters
Try to cram their tired bodies into the already full carriage.
One of them cradles coffee in a plastic cup,
Protecting it like a mother protecting her baby.
Distant music of the peddlers begging for a penny
Reach the commuters' ears.
As the doors slide shut,
An announcement is caught from the computer voice
Which the employees hear every day.
Then the tube stirs and moves off on its daily rounds.
Forever cursed to follow in its footsteps.

Katrin Duffill-Telsnig (13)
The Harrodian School, Barnes

Being Lost

(Inspired by EE Cummings style of writing)

ScAry is BeIng Lost
BeIng Lost is Dark and gloomy
BeIng Lost is nOt good?
BeIng Lost can torture and hurt
Lost can scar for life
TeRRifying is BeIng Lost
BeIng Lost Is bAd.

Alex Koukov (11)
The Harrodian School, Barnes

A Star's View

I see the galaxy
and think, am I ever going to move?

I see my children,
my moons, smiling at me, orbiting me.

I see my mother,
the sun, shining rays of light.

I notice a planet with colours,
life,
it's real.

My light is dying, I'm moving on,
no danger has ever come to me,
my children move with me.

I'm gone!

Ella Loudon (11)
The Harrodian School, Barnes

The Autumn Tree

When I was small,
The first thing that I saw in a park
Was this thick, long, brown, hard and very tall plant.
It had green, yellow, red and orange leaves
Hanging off this plant.
My dad suddenly picked me up
And put me on the plant.
I felt like I was the biggest person on Earth.
A bit like a giant.
I also felt like I was on top of the world.
Then I asked my dad,
'What is the plant's name?'
He said, 'It's called a tree
And the leaves change colour in the autumn.'

Amy Boisseau (12)
The Harrodian School, Barnes

In Japan

(Inspired by Cesca Cooke)

In Japan
The secrets are all hidden

In Japan
The clothes are made of linen

In Japan
The cherry blossom grows

In Japan
The beautiful water flows

In Japan
Lights bob along the riverbanks

In Japan
The sushi is kept in tanks

In Japan
The dragons roam

In Japan
There is my home.

Sara Allen (12)
The Harrodian School, Barnes

Beneath The Surface

Another crisp day,
Sun beaming,
The sound of a trickling stream.
She daren't breathe,
As she may be heard.
She removes her long dress
And slips into the deep blue lake.
She submerges
Underwater,
Never to be seen again.

Tijan Siddiqi (13)
The Harrodian School, Barnes

Autumn's Colours

When the sky grows dark so early
The leaves turn gold
And the skies turn pearly
The year grows old.

The wind whips along the streets
Brushing against our faces
Children cry trick or treats
Wet leaves pile up in empty spaces.

This is a season of long forgotten
What comes in spring
Leaves in autumn
A cold wind winter will bring.

No colour, no sun
All the leaves have gone
The Earth is done
Soon winter will come.

Ella Chevasco (12)
The Harrodian School, Barnes

Hell's Blessing

Death be unto this place
Plague be unto its men
Light from above reverts
To leave this forsaken wilderness

Of destruction blessed naught
And cheeping of doom
Leave this place with a boon
To supply its horror
And dole out its fright
Do not sink low
Go above to the blessed light.

Max Dampier (13)
The Harrodian School, Barnes

Alone In New York

I stepped out of the airport, into a new world,
Towering buildings and crowded streets,
Smelling the polluted air from the cars on the streets,
Alone and afraid in New York.

I walked along the sidewalk, hearing the horns
From the cars stuck in a gridlock.
I saw a clock. Tick-tock, tick-tock,
Alone and afraid in New York.

I walked down a back alley and saw five boys,
They came over to me and started to sneer.
One of them threw a punch, hit me in the ear,
Alone and afraid in New York.

When the police found me, I was on the floor,
Stab wounds in my back,
Dead as a sack,
Alone and afraid in New York.

William Essayan (12)
The Harrodian School, Barnes

Chinatown

Lots of lights and Chinese people
XXX shops and Siamese people
Cantonese writing and drunken fighting
The sound of a thousand cigarettes lighting
Lots of little markets and rock 'n' roll stores
On most corners stand Japanese whores
Car horns beeping and people eating
The sizzle of a wok pan, a happy Asian chef man
The wind is bitter on your cold face
So you try to find a little warm place
If you want a bit to eat
Buy some vegetables on the street
I stand in the middle and wear a crown
There is no frown in Chinatown.

Rupert Simonian (13)
The Harrodian School, Barnes

The Wintertime

I sit in my living room
And watch the winter arrive
Through my crystal clear window
I see the snowflakes that drop

There the ice covers all the buildings
And the snow that goes right on top
I see the freezing people pass
And enjoy my comfort in my home

I press my hand against the window
And leave it there for a while
Then I turn around and go
Slowly I walk away

I rest on my nice warm sofa
And listen to the roaring fire
I hold my hot chocolate in my hand
Then look outside again

I see the shiny icicles
With very pointy ends
There it hangs, so tightly
The sharp ice is frozen on

My radiator heating the house
I feel so warm and cosy
I rest my eyes and think to myself
How wonderful the winter really is

I turn to the window again
And remember there was a puddle
In the rusty autumn days
And see that it has frozen now
So frosty, yet so full of beauty.

Lara Al-Sabti (12)
The Harrodian School, Barnes

Last Gasp

Beckham has the ball
He gives it to me
I hear a call
So I pass to Rooney

He passes it back
I run to the ball
I give it a crack
Then I hear a call

I hit it my best
It goes in with a crash
The goalie fails his test
Hits the ground with a smash

It's the very last minute
The best time to score
Out of the keeper's limit
The crowd screams for more

I am the captain of the team
I go up for the cup
It's a glorious dream
As I lift it up

The lads and me
Celebrate in joy
A great game to see
We had worked our ploy

The Queen shakes my hand
And says, 'Well done, boy'
The whole of the land
Is jumping for joy

I lift up the cup
        And I wake up.

Harry Forte (12)
The Harrodian School, Barnes

Africa

Across the dry plains of Africa
The cheetah sprints for his prey
Across the dry plains of Africa
The vulture is busy all day.

The lion sleeps in the shade of the tree
Hidden from everyone
He sits there still, where no one can see him
His belly full, his prey gone.

Across the dry plains of Africa
The elephant swings his tail
Trying to stay cool, he finds water
Marks on his tusks tell his tale.

Across the dry plains of Africa
The sun goes down in the west
The wind blows through the Kigelia
Under the trees the animals rest.

Across the dry plains of Africa
The stars and the moon shine bright
The leopard hunts the impala
The hyena gives him a fright.

Across the night sky of Africa
My heart begins to race
Because when I think of Africa
There can't be a better place.

Francesca Cooke (12)
The Harrodian School, Barnes

My Grandad

I'm lucky to have my grandad,
My nickname for him is 'fun dad'.

He took us to 'Noise's Off',
And we weren't allowed to cough.

But I was laughing so much, I had to shout,
So they picked me up and sent me out.

In the corridor I fell to the floor,
And cried, 'Please, please, no more, no more!'

My mouth was wide open,
My eyes bulging,
My ears began steaming,
My nose smoking.

As soon as I could I went back inside,
Thinking my laughter had finally died.
Then Gary started tumbling down the stairs,
'Cause he thought Dotty was having affairs.

And I burst out laughing again,
Till I was sobbing with the pain.
Then I sat down, but missed my seat,
And *wheee!* up in the air went my feet!

And that was the end of the show.

So thank you, Grandad,
For being such a great fun dad!

Finn Harries (11)
The Harrodian School, Barnes

Cricket

The toss is thrown by their captain
Who wants to bat first
But our hopes are up to bowl
You can't bat in heat like this, we need to quench our thirst.

The first ball is a four
The second is a single
Their batsmen are very fast
But ours are very nimble.

We stop halfway to eat
In our suncream and our hats
The other team come in exhausted
Too tired to hold their bats.

We finish the match
With one hundred and four
After our ninth batsman
Slipped and hit the floor.

We end the day joyfully
With celebrations and cheers
But sadly there's no chance
Of having a pint of beer.

Raf Cross (11)
The Harrodian School, Barnes

The Traffic Junction

Squealing to a halt, the cars slow at the deciding beam
                                    of the traffic light,
waiting for it to change from red, to orange, to green.
The cars have come to a complete standstill,
their red brake lights adding to the red glare of the traffic lights.
Cars are squashed together like sardines in a tin.

Someone honks their horn, adding to the din,
music pumping through an open window,
like a thousand soldiers running across a plain.
The loud clatter of the builders replacing the tarmac,
so hot that I could almost taste it.
And finally the purr of awaiting car engines ready to leap into action.

The acrid smell of the car fumes expel out of the exhausts
like water pouring out of the drainpipe,
ready to jump up and swallow me whole.
I stand there feeling the hot, stinking fumes billow up and around me,
as if waiting for the right moment to overcome me.

The red turns to orange,
so the waiting cars, whose drivers were waiting intently
                                    watching for green, depart.
The red vanishes and with it the cars, until the red returns again.

Holly Hough (13)
The Harrodian School, Barnes

The Scorpion

As the black image emerges
From under the rock
The human approaches
With caution.

The black image scuttles
Towards the human
Like tumbleweed in a soft breeze.
He freezes.

And suddenly
The scorpion jumps like a spring
And clings onto the man
Violently shaking his arm to get
The scorpion off.

The scorpion wounds the man's arm
With its strong, crab-like claws
And its tail unravels like a party blower
And the sharp spike is injected like a needle.

The poison shoots . . .
The man falls to his death.

Gabriel Bean (11)
The Harrodian School, Barnes

Thoughts Of A Broken Heart (Rap)

I'm lying in my bed,
Crying because I miss you,
The only thought in my head,
Is being back with you,
As I wipe my tears with a tissue,
I reminisce about the time when I used to hug and kiss you.

But I know that those times are over,
I should never have given you the cold shoulder,
Correcting myself over, the things I should have told her,
Before that man swooped in and stole her.

And now my heart is hollow
And I'm left to wallow,
In my sorrow,
Hoping that she'll be by my side tomorrow.

But I know it won't come true,
I wonder if you think about me, the way I think about you,
I wonder if you would take me back if I poured my heart out to you,
Because I'll do anything to make it up to you.

Omar Mooro (12)
The Harrodian School, Barnes

Chocolate

C hocolate, who doesn't like it?
H azelnuts crunch between teeth,
O val-shaped sections melt in mouths,
C hocolate, who doesn't like it?
O nce you have sampled it, you succumb to the
L uxurious delight that fills your mouth,
A ll shapes and tastes fill the bite but one
T ransfixed colour, brown, dark brown.
E xcept for Smarties, they're different.

Eshaa Sharma (14)
The Lady Eleanor Holles School, Hampton

Rebelling

Today I'll put my brother's toothbrush down the toilet.
I'll leave the top off the toothpaste.
Today I'll throw my duvet on the floor.
I won't put my dirty washing in the washing basket.
Today I'll have a cookie dough ice cream for breakfast.
I'll eat all the biscuits out of the barrel.
Today I'll get a different bus and go shopping instead.
I'll buy lots of tops with my belly sticking out.
Today I will buy 50 cats.
I'll develop a nervous twitch at the dinner table.
Today I'll throw homework sheets out of the window.
I'll listen to loud music all night.
Now I'm going to ask my parents for lots of money
And they are going to say, 'No!'

Charlotte Perkins (12)
The Lady Eleanor Holles School, Hampton

Birthday Cake

To round off the meal, is this birthday treat
Wonderfully sticky and rich and sweet.
I blow out the candles while my friends cheer,
One more candle since it happened last year.
I ready the knife to plunge into the cake,
That only this morning my mother did bake.
I cut the first slice, people reach for the plate,
Impatient, they grab, not wanting to wait.
The aroma of chocolate reaches my nose,
I can't wait to eat the cake that I chose.
We bite into the cake, so rich and moist
And after a moment our pleasure is voiced.
We munch at the cake and before too long,
We sadly discover, that the cake's all gone.

Emma Newman (14)
The Lady Eleanor Holles School, Hampton

A Trifling Tale

(Dedicated to my godmother whose true experience was the inspiration for this poem)

My mother made a trifle to eat on Christmas Day
And this poem tells the trifle's fate when Granny came to stay . . .

The sponge and jam and berries were in layers of gold and red,
With a pale, runny 'crème vanille' that glistened as it spread.
The only layer left to add was cream, but not just yet;
Mum said she'd whip it later, once the 'crème vanille' had set.

Now Granny was in earshot and heard the creamy plan
And offered up her expertise as only Granny can.
Mum said she needn't worry as the whipping stage was planned,
But Granny thought in any case she'd lend a helping hand.

So when Mum nipped out for almonds to the local village shop;
(Remember you need toasted nuts to decorate the top),
Granny saw her chance to help and thought it would be good
To whip the cream, two pints of it and finish off the pud.

What Granny hadn't bargained for, was electronic power,
As our new electric beaters whisk at 90 miles an hour.
In a flash the cream had clotted to a butter-yellow paste,
But Granny still decided that it shouldn't go to waste.

Although the cream was far too thick, she didn't think it mattered
And she'd more or less cleaned up the walls where
                          whipping cream had splattered.
So with the cream and knife, she then performed the operation
And when the cream was all blobbed on, felt Granny-type elation.

In truth the cream had lifted all the layers one by one,
'Til the trifle was a mushy mess and all the layers had gone.
The clear glass bowl that previously had shone with red and gold,
Was playing host to mixed up gunge that now looked grey and old.

She sensed the bowl did not show off the pud to best effect.
Even Granny must have realised that by now the layers were wrecked.
So ever-optimistic, Granny found a large blue pot
And she turned the glass bowl upside down and then tipped in the lot.

Granny bravely soldiered on and found the glacé cherries.
Much more Christmassy than nuts she mused;
they look like holly berries.
When Mum returned, the sight before her gave her quite a start,
As Granny proudly waved her hands towards her work of art.

In fact, at first, Mum didn't twig that this pot held her trifle
And when she did, she gasped and then said words
that she should stifle.
I felt so sad for Mum though, as she hid her face and cried,
But it seems her tears were laughter as she rocked from side to side.

The trifle now the worse for wear had taken quite a beating.
It resembled our dog's dinner, Mum said, not for human eating.
However, Christmas evening, with the trifle on the table,
Granny spooned it out and ate as much as she was able.

Then said the blue pot wasn't right when a portion had been taken.
So she found a nice big Tupperware, into which the pud was shaken.
By now we were quite speechless as we all had been so sure
There was no further punishment this trifle could endure.

This trifling tale is always told at Christmas every year
And at the Tupperware container bit, we all let out a cheer!
Mum still makes her trifle for the tea on Christmas Day
And we all make sure that Granny is kept well out of the way!

Daisy Perrin (14)
The Lady Eleanor Holles School, Hampton

A Chocolate Dream

I lie down and I ponder,
Into my dream I wander,
Trees of sweets
And lakes of sauce -
Chocolate, of course,
Fields of crisps,
Liquorice bark,
A cascade of sherbet
That glows in the dark.

Strawberry laces,
That dangle from trees,
A door made of pizza,
Who knows where it leads?

I walk into a house,
Some people are there,
They are gingerbread men,
With long, orange hair.

The people, they greet,
But I'd rather eat,
So I go to the bookcase
And pick out some sweets.

I feel myself getting bigger,
It must be the chocolate finger,
I swirl into another world,
With apples and pears, but no chocolate twirls.

My dream is a nightmare,
No longer tasty treats,
I wake up in a hurry
And I . . . need . . . sweets.

Arabella Burfitt-Dons (12)
The Lady Eleanor Holles School, Hampton

The First Day Back

Thursday morning in September
Is a day we'd all remember.

School was due to start again
Alarm clocks ringing made that plain.

Sombre clothing, black and grey
Was the order of the day.

Sports bag, school bag, file and all
Stood there waiting in the hall.

Breakfast just did not appeal
As scared and nervous I did feel.

I tossed and turned the whole night through
And now departure time was due.

Though at home I'd rather stay
To the car I made my way.

All too soon the school appeared
Less alarming than I'd feared.

In the classroom found my seat
Once again with friends to meet.

Holiday tales were being told
Amazing adventures to unfold.

The noise was silenced by the bell
The teacher now appeared as well.

Greeting all with smiling face
Each girl seated in her place.

Little's changed it's much the same
Just the class has a different name.

Laavanya Selvarajah (12)
The Lady Eleanor Holles School, Hampton

It's All About The Punch

The colour of raw steak,
With a small splash of mustard.
Or maybe it's blackberries,
With a little drop of custard.

Before the bell rang,
The two fighters were standing.
Who'd have seen coming
Such a rough landing?

A left and a right,
An up and a down.
A bob and a weave,
A cheer then a frown.

All squinty and blurred,
The sight's not the same.
The eye was just perfect,
Before the fist came.

Florence Parrack (12)
The Lady Eleanor Holles School, Hampton

Space Toaster

My kitchen toaster is so clean,
It looks like a silver space machine!
With lift up seats and red-hot power,
We'd get to space in half an hour!

I'll push down the button and off we'll go,
We'll shoot up high through rain and snow!
Me, my friends and the space toaster,
Moving like a roller coaster!

But now our trip is at an end,
We're going round our very last bend!
We're coming down to Earth in time,
To see the toast popping out of this rhyme!

Cecilia Long (11)
The Lady Eleanor Holles School, Hampton

Hunter

The dusty creature crouches in the sun,
It looks around searching for the one.
Its paws beat down on the grassy ground,
Making sure not to make a sound.
Its eyes dart across the arid plain,
Finding food will keep it sane.
The hunter starts to roar and growl,
Starving always makes him howl.
Its hair stands up as it senses prey,
It's had anticipation throughout the whole day.
Then, in a sudden, up it leaps,
Soon the prey will be for keeps.
The race is on! Off the hunter goes,
Will he catch the deer? No one knows.
From the bush, the sound of clicks,
Is the hunter now the hunted, or could his mind be playing tricks?

Eshana Subherwal (12)
The Lady Eleanor Holles School, Hampton

Bluebells

So luscious yet so wondrous,
The bluebells stand graciously, waiting for me to see.
Innocently I watch them, ponderous
I see them staring at me.

They were demure in an ominous wood,
Their petals topsy-turvy trumpets,
Heralding the coming of ebullient spring,
Inviting me to frolic and play them in a flamboyant way.

Their petals are overturned cups,
Dripping sweet fairy juice every day.
A terrestrial carpet of blue they wove,
In the titillating sunshine.

Roxanne Bamford (14)
The Lady Eleanor Holles School, Hampton

The Bad Day

Today, I will not feel lucky
And I will not grab the opportunity,
Today, I will do whatever I please,
I will not bother to take constructive criticism,
I will dwell on my hardship,
I will not persevere
And not be open to new experiences or tasks.

Instead

I will indulge in my misfortune,
I will cry for my loneliness
And drown in a pool of tears,
I will get comfort from my self pity
And jump with rage and fury,
I will survive on nothing but my past,
Until my mood passes and my memory fades,
As a new sun rises,
A new day is born.

Priyanka Shaunak (12)
The Lady Eleanor Holles School, Hampton

Packed Lunches

Locked in my locker, tucked safely away
Are cold, clammy sandwiches from yesterday
Bursting with cheese and Parma ham
Mingled with mould from Sunday's roast lamb.

Squidged in the corner next to the grapes
Lies the banana with scratches and scrapes.

On top of the sandwiches covered in juice
Is Mum's favourite recipe home-made mousse.

All these surprises lie waiting for me
When at last I unearth my locker key.

Anna Sparrow (11)
The Lady Eleanor Holles School, Hampton

A Sunset Walk In The 'Gorges De Véroncle'

Towering cliffs and hollowed caves
Look down upon the stony waves,
Formed by the river in the gorge,
Lined with watermill and forge.

The cliff tops bask in dusk's red light,
While down below, already night
Is cooling rocks of daytime heat,
Still warm and dry beneath our feet.

Lizards rustle through the leaves,
Bats emerge from rotted eaves,
The noise of insects slowly dies,
As a lonesome buzzard cries.

Scrambling over stony walls
We slip and slide as darkness falls,
Then tired at last we turn and run,
As if to catch the fading sun.

Antonia Millard (12)
The Lady Eleanor Holles School, Hampton

Rambutans

Rambutans
Prickly red skin
Tentacles like a sea urchin
Nestling deep in the fruit bowl
Inviting your fingers to stroke them out
Peel springs off and juicy fruit appears
Pale as a skinless orange segment
One bite of liquid softness
Fresh and aromatic
Rambutans.

Emma Linthwaite (12)
The Lady Eleanor Holles School, Hampton

Frustration

Today I will not listen to anyone who talks to me,
I will not do what people say,
But I will do whatever I want.
I will say things that I don't mean
And no one can tell me off.

I will wear whatever I feel like,
Buy all of the best things in the shops
And I am going to fight as much as I want with my brother.
But most of all, I won't get into trouble for things I didn't do.
I will also eat lots and lots of chocolate.

I think I will write on all of the white boards at school:
'I am the best!' in red ink too.
I think I might even push people into the swimming pool.
I am going to be a wild child.

Aarti Sood (12)
The Lady Eleanor Holles School, Hampton

My Loved One

I sit by you and watch you go away
I think of the things we did together
When we were children and we used to play
In rain or snow, whatever the weather.
Why did you have to leave me alone here?
As I look to the sky and think of you
I think of all the times that you were near
I will live my life for me and you too.
I wish I had been there when you had gone
I would have told you it would be all right
Some time we will play again, all day long
Never will you have to struggle and fight.
In memory of you, there is a tree,
For evermore, your soul will be with me.

Laura Martin (14)
The Lady Eleanor Holles School, Hampton

Food

Crumpets with butter and fresh cups of coffee,
Cheesecake and tartlets and whipped cream banoffee;
Jacket potatoes when we're in the mood.
These are a few of our favourite foods.

Cans full of olives and sticky spaghetti
Cold chicken salad, Italian confetti,
All of these nibbles make stomachs protrude,
But we don't mind - they're our favourite foods!

Rich bowls of fried rice with lashings of sauce,
Heinz tomato ketchup is mentioned of course!
Sunday roast dinners we mustn't exclude.
These are a few of our favourite foods.

When we're hungry
When we're starving
When we're feeling sad.

We simply remember our favourite foods
And then we don't feel so bad!

Joanna Markbreiter (12)
The Lady Eleanor Holles School, Hampton

School Dinners

I stand outside the big, wooden door,
An uneasy feeling, as I stare at the floor,
The lunch menu stands as a testament to all,
Enter at your own risk, into this hall,
Teachers allow you through one at a time,
Which option to choose, which line?

The hall reeks of fish and stale food,
Nothing in the hall satisfies my mood,
But I get into the queue for curry and rice,
Grab a plate, fork and knife,
I sit at a table with my friends,
Eating the *food* until lunchtime ends.

When it comes down to lunch, what can I say?
Inedible food is served every day.
Also, I have a feeling that what we don't eat,
Reappears on the menu as a mystery meat.
Next term I think I should make my own,
Lunch will be safer, if I make it at home!

Helen Pye (13)
The Lady Eleanor Holles School, Hampton

Mushrooms

The smell of spaghetti Bolognese is wafting from the kitchen,
Mum knows I hate mushrooms,
But I bet she has put them in!
She cuts them up so small,
She thinks I do not know they are there!
But I do.

Those little, black, slimy creatures,
Lurking amongst the delicious pools of tomato sauce.
'Dinner's ready!'
A voice calls from the kitchen,
Even from sitting on the wooden kitchen chair,
I can see them; I know they are there.

How can anybody like these 'things'?
They seem to be growing everywhere.
Toadstools in the garden,
Fungi on the trees,
Mushrooms all around me,
They are even in my tea!

Bethan George (12)
The Lady Eleanor Holles School, Hampton

I Wonder

I wonder what it would be like to be famous . . .
Having to be groomed to perfection,
Always living in the limelight -
I'd forget what is real and what is not.

I wonder what it would be like to be an extreme sportsman . . .
Soaring the sky with my glider,
Swooping down slopes on skis,
Catching waves with my surfboard.

I wonder what it would be like to be a doctor . . .
People having to place their trust in me,
Counting on me to break the pain,
A lifesaver, hero, most of the time.

I wonder what it would be like to be homeless . . .
Living life on an unnamed kerb,
No money, no warmth, no love,
Not noticed, tucked in a doorway, alone.

I wonder.

Jemima Benstead (13)
The Lady Eleanor Holles School, Hampton

Rebel

To annoy my family today,
I will switch the salt and sugar,
Or put biscuit crumbs in my brother's bed.

To be a pain today,
I will make a snide comment,
Or taunt my brother.

To make my mum mad today,
I will not tidy my room,
Or I will lose my mobile phone.

To make my teacher angry today,
I'll muck around in lessons,
Or chat to my friends.

To annoy everyone at school today,
I will skip the lunch queue,
Or leave rubbish in my form room.

But tomorrow,
Maybe I'll behave,
Maybe . . .

Kirsty Dixon (12)
The Lady Eleanor Holles School, Hampton

Ahead Of Our Time

Many thousands of years ago, when people first came along,
They were what we call uncivilised and did things we now think wrong.

They didn't know about farming, but of course, they had to eat,
So it seems quite reasonable to me that they lived on nothing but
meat.

We say the Romans and the Greeks were the beginnings of civilisation,
But they did things that now would cause a worldwide revolution.

By then they knew about farming and growing things to eat,
We say this discovery changed the world, but they went on eating
meat.

Then the world slid into a dark age, where society went insane,
And people did many hundreds of things that we call inhumane.

And I suppose since it was the Dark Age, it's really quite all right
That when it comes to eating meat, they didn't see the light.

But after many centuries, the modern era began,
And people saw that doing what's right is the duty of every man.

And then some people realised how wrong it was to feed
Themselves on helpless animals, but hardly anyone agreed.

But maybe in the future, people will have stopped this crime,
Maybe we vegetarians are simply ahead of our time.

Emily Hertz (14)
The Lady Eleanor Holles School, Hampton

School Dinners

'Attention class, form an orderly queue,
Stop pushing, there is plenty of food for all of you!'
Yelled the dinner lady, handing out plates.
I think school dinners are absolutely great!
Pizza, pasta, chocolate sponge cake,
Ice cream, lasagne, vegetable bake,
Toad-in-the-hole, shepherd's pie,
Jelly or pancakes stacked up high.
Fish fingers, burgers and lots of chips,
Jam doughnuts, licking the lips.
For school dinners I am never late,
I think they're absolutely great!

'Quiet class, that means you too!
Today's special is broccoli stew!'
The shoving stops, the class sighs,
Nobody wants to be first in line!
I remember the poster on the notice board,
'Why is obesity a crime Lord?'
It's healthy eating from now on,
The junk food days have disappeared and gone!
'Now school dinners aren't that great,
In fact, it's one of the things I absolutely *hate!*'

Jasmine Gupta (12)
The Lady Eleanor Holles School, Hampton

Spider's Web

I see a web being spun by a spider
The web - like magic - comes from inside her
She spins and spins, like a possessed one
Until the enticing web is done.

I see her scurry off to one side
She watches and waits for a meal with pride
Until something unwary gets stuck - a fly
It is glued to the web - it is waiting to die.

Suddenly - on the web - a hand comes down
The perpetrator's punishment is only my frown
A complex, time-consuming web
Ruined - with the two lives that away did ebb.

I sit a while in that place and think
Could intricate work be destroyed in a blink?
My thoughts wander to the death of my wife
And see the connection between the web and life.

Her life was destroyed in a simple car crash
And think how the web fell from my son's slash
Both so complicated, so (apparently) strong
Both in one action, suddenly gone.

Anna Comboni (12)
The Lady Eleanor Holles School, Hampton

The Bowl

The large, empty bowl stares absently across its shiny,
untouched surface
But the sieving of self-raising flour sends a troop of tiny white balls
To descend on its territory, to destroy the spotless expanse.
Soon after, three giant lumps of butter hurl through the air
onto the bowl.
A crack of an egg sends a warm, orange goo oozing into the mixture
Dipping and rising across the vast stretch of the bowl.
The sprinkling of caster sugar floats delicately onto the floor,
Eggs and butter like small, dainty snowflakes falling through the sky.
A drop of vanilla essence brings colour and vibrance to the dull mixture
And a pinch of baking powder brings flavour.

The ruthless, wooden spoon then whips rapidly in and out of the bowl
Making the mixture smooth and flawless.
Next, it is placed in the oven where it bakes from milky-white
to golden brown.
The mixture is banished and the cake is produced.
Its warm, rich smell forces its way out and ascends through the air.
The bowl is now forgotten about and put back in its dingy,
dark cupboard
Where it waits again for its time.

Anna Reilly (14)
The Lady Eleanor Holles School, Hampton

School Dinners

Finally, the bell sounds throughout the school
And everyone knows that this means lunch calls!
The thumping of elephants gets louder,
Like greyhounds racing, we mustn't flounder!

Rumbling stomachs from the majority,
School lunch is, of course, our priority.
Pushing and shoving, all of us want food,
Otherwise we will be in a bad mood!

Minutes have passed by, waiting in the queue,
Will I be the next lucky one let through?
'Please Miss, I've been waiting longer than her!'
'That's so unfair, she pushed in back there, Sir!'

Starved and exhausted, I reach the lunch hall,
Main course and pudding, I would like it all!
Who knows how much more of this I can take?
There is no end to this, more queues await!

Not knowing what food is left, I don't care!
I am so hungry, I could eat a bear!
As long as my stomach is silenced soon,
I will devour whatever greets my spoon.

Sarah Melotte (14)
The Lady Eleanor Holles School, Hampton

Today . . .

Today I will leave ladders in my tights.
Today my shirt will be untucked.
Today I will sprint through the corridors.
Today I will stand on my desk and scream.
      I will not listen to others.

Today I will put my rubbish on the floor.
Today I will leave it there.
Today I will have my mobile on in lessons.
Today I will text no one.
      But pretend my phone is ringing.

Today I will knock on the head teacher's door
And run away.
Today I will rip up my books.
Today I will blame it on the dog.
Today I will cover up my ears when my friends are talking
                about something incredibly boring.
   Blah! Blah! Blah!

Today I will 'accidentally' forget my homework.
I will climb over the school fence
      And run, for life.

Nida Khan (12)
The Lady Eleanor Holles School, Hampton

Junk Food Baby

When I was younger,
I'm surprised I did not starve of hunger!
I cannot believe the things they fed me,
Who on Earth wants mushed banana for tea?

Well, it didn't stop my mum from feeding it to me!
I think I ate it up until the age of three!
And when she told me that processed broccoli was my favourite of all,
I said, 'No way! I bet I would have preferred even a fur ball!'

However, it did not stop there!
I must have been in despair!
Mashed avocado and baby rice,
Why couldn't they have fed me something nice?

They could have fed me chips and sweets,
All the yummy little treats,
Did they not know that I would have done anything for some chips
And to feel their tasty flavour on my lips?

I suppose it was all for my own good,
They did all they could,
Could they not have at least given me some chocolate, just maybe?
However, I don't think I would have liked to be a junk food baby!

Katie-Jane Sullivan (12)
The Lady Eleanor Holles School, Hampton

Time For Tea!

I don't think I'll get up from the sofa,
I like it here.
I don't think I'll turn off the TV,
I like watching the 'X-Factor'.
I don't want to get the knives from the drawer,
The knives are sharp you know.
I don't want to lay the table,
Knives on the right, forks on the left?
I don't want to be the person who serves the food,
I want to eat it instead.
The waft of the roast, the potatoes, the gravy . . .
I don't want to listen to my dad going on and on about politics,
It's all boring to me.
'I don't want to do the washing-up, I did it last time!'
'But it's your turn to do it!'
'It's been my turn for the last two weeks!'

I won't go to the table today,
I'm going to sit here and do nothing.

I don't think Mum's going to offer me dinner,
I can smell the roast.
I'm hungry,
I think I should go and lay the table.

Susie Chaytow (12)
The Lady Eleanor Holles School, Hampton

I Loathe

I loathe the way we are run by the government,
We are ants under their fist of power.
I loathe the way we cannot have our say,
No one listens to children.
I loathe the way children are treated differently,
We are not equal with teachers.
I loathe the way people interrupt you when you are speaking
And then you cannot say anything because they are talking.
I loathe the way people expect so much of you
And when you fail, people do not accept the fact that you tried.
I loathe the way we are powerless to do anything,
The way that someone starts a war and we are powerless to stop it.
I loathe the way it is so easy to become a celebrity,
You can sell a made-up story to a newspaper and you are famous.
I loathe the way we are taxed
And the government does not even put the money to good use.
I loathe the way people sue each other for the smallest of things,
If you make one wrong move, you will end up in court.
But there are many things I loathe about the world
And people often forget what they like about it.
We take things for granted
And in a world of different opinions,
There is no right or wrong,
Just an answer.

Kate Smith (12)
The Lady Eleanor Holles School, Hampton

Heartbreak

When love is hard
And dreams aren't found
Your heart breaks
And tries to sing its song.

It tells you how
You're meant to feel
It tells you how
Your love is dear.

And when that love
Seems hard to find
Look inside
And solve the rhyme.

And when you've solved
That jigsaw puzzle
Your heart will mend
Without a trouble.

When love is sweet
And dreams are calm
Your heart awakes
And sings its song.

Nagham Al-Turaihi (12)
The Lady Eleanor Holles School, Hampton

This And That

I don't want to do this,
I don't want to do that.
I'm late for this and that,
I'm bored.

I hate getting up early,
I'm going back to bed.
I won't turn up,
For this or that,
Who cares?

I hate double this thats,
This and that, back to back.
I can't stop working
For a chat.

I hate that assembly,
I hate sitting on the floor.
Even my feet have fallen asleep,
I can't stand this or that anymore.

Most of all I hate
Doing this and that
All the time.
I can't wait till I'm eighteen
And don't have to do this or that anymore.

Katherine Courtis (12)
The Lady Eleanor Holles School, Hampton

Love Of Food

Food is about:

Eating the froth off the top of a cappuccino,
And then leaving the coffee.
Chasing the last pea around your plate,
And then picking it up with your fingers and eating it.
Buying a hot chocolate,
Just so you can eat the biscuit that comes with it.

Food is about:

Licking the ice cream as it runs down your cone,
Only eating the icing that covers your slice of cake,
Eating the chocolate but leaving the nut inside,
Fighting over who will be the one to eat the last piece of chicken
                                          at the dinner table.

Food is about:

Sucking the sweets,
But crunching them before you have finished them.
Twirling a strand of spaghetti around your fork,
When it feels like it is never going to end.
Slurping your soup off the spoon,
Even though you know it annoys your mother.

But food is sensory pleasure on a plate.

Rhian Wood (14)
The Lady Eleanor Holles School, Hampton

My Strawberry

A warm, red, sophisticated glow.
A subtle hint of summertime,
The sweet aroma of the sparkling sunshine.
The scrumptious taste of Heaven on Earth.

My strawberry looks like a baby rosebud,
Waiting to show the world its precious petals.
It is like an old-fashioned sweet,
Colourful, appetising, delicious and sickly.

My strawberry smells of a warm, pleasant day,
The days that were filled with happiness.
It smells of grass after it has rained
And flowers at the peak of their short-lived lives.

My strawberry feels like a heart-shaped, red quilt,
Overstuffed and studded with golden pips.
It feels like a silky smooth feather,
Falling through the buoyant air.

My strawberry sounds like adorable, charming baby birds,
Chirruping for their good-natured mothers.
It sounds like the warm, summery breeze,
Snaking its way through the whispery grasses.

My strawberry tastes like an expensive chocolate,
Hard and crunchy on the outside, yet creamy on the inside.
It tastes like a country garden,
Irresistible, luscious, attractive and dainty.

Georgina Bale (12)
The Lady Eleanor Holles School, Hampton

Chocolate

My operation had finished
And I was feeling very battered.
Hospital food is not the most delicious food in the world,
You must agree.

So, my mother went to the canteen,
While I was being pestered by the nurse
And bought me a little treat.

It was a chocolate bar.

Being a sensible girl as I was,
I bit into the bar slowly,
Just to make that taste last.

Joy rushed up my spine
And I took another bite.

The sweet flooded in
And I felt all warm inside.
You see, I had not eaten before my operation
And I was very, very hungry.

The happiness lasted for a few more minutes,
Till I was hungry again
And urging for another sugar rush.

In the end, I made do
With lumpy, boring mashed potato
And slimy macaroni cheese.

Sarika Sharma (12)
The Lady Eleanor Holles School, Hampton

Oh, To Be A Rebel!

That's it! I've had enough!
Today I just won't care.
I shall ignore the alarm, wear my skirt too short,
Won't even brush my hair!

I'll shun the fruit and cereal,
Eat chocolate chip ice cream.
I shall leave for school at half-past eight,
The bus goes at eight-fifteen!

I'll leave my homework by the bed,
It's orange slips for me.
I'll make some noise, talk to boys
And act outrageously!

I shall fidget in class and talk and laugh,
Tell jokes to my friends and be funny
And then daydream of shopping down Rodeo Drive,
With my dad, spending all of his money!

I shall play lacrosse all afternoon,
Ten goals would be so sweet.
Then I'll ban other girls from the changing room,
Well, the ones with smelly feet!

On the way home, I'll text my dad
And say how bad I've been.
He'll send me to bed without any tea,
Just wait till I'm eighteen!

Grace Warwick (12)
The Lady Eleanor Holles School, Hampton

Are You The Food You Eat?

People say you are the food you eat,
Does my sister remind you of a chocolate treat?
I have looked at her every day,
Does she seem to have changed in any way?

People say you are the food you eat,
When a family of bears she did meet
And returning from a little forage,
Did Goldilocks look like a bowl of porridge?

People say you are the food you eat,
But as Miss Muffett sprang to her feet,
And she quickly ran away,
Did she start to look like curds and whey?

People say you are the food you eat,
When in the corner Jack did seat
And pulled from a pie, a plum,
I could see no change, even in his thumb.

People say you are the food you eat,
When Eve with the apple she did cheat,
Despite being the apple of Adam's eye,
Did she become an apple within a pie?

People say you are the food you eat,
But I think it would be quite a feat,
For me to change into Cadbury's Flakes,
Or even a packet of Jaffa Cakes.

Natalie Keeler (14)
The Lady Eleanor Holles School, Hampton

A Hula Hoop Banana Man

Yesterday I had
A banana for break,
A boring, old banana
And it was squished.
I wish I was like Sally,
She gets a pound for the tuck shop every day
And Harriet gets a double choc-chip Smarties cookie every day,
But for me it's a squashed banana.
Jenny had Hula Hoops,
Lucky girl,
'Give me one, Jen?' I begged,
Jenny drew a Hula Hoop from the red bag
And stuck it on my banana,
I was startled, but she just kept going,
She drew two more Hula Hoops from the pack
And stuck them on either side of my banana,
'Jen,' I cried, 'What have you done?'
She replied, 'Well, can't you see?
It's the Hula Hoop banana man.'
So I discovered bananas can be as interesting as you want them to be,
Even Harriet stopped guzzling her cookie
To see the banana man boogie.
So bananas can be interesting;
If you don't believe me,
Try it yourself.

Stephanie MacAulay (12)
The Lady Eleanor Holles School, Hampton

The Strange Night

One strange and quiet, starry night
While the children were asleep,
I saw a spacecraft landing
In the field, beside the creek.

I saw three creatures standing
In the bright light of the moon,
Some of them were smiling
Others whistling a strange tune.

They all adventured into town
Where people stopped to stare,
For it is rarely we get visitors
With six eyes and yellow hair.

Soon it was in the papers
And all over the TV,
That men from Mars had landed
And many rushed to see.

They were trapped in chains and padlocks
And made to quake with fear,
So in a cloud of smoke and dust
They quickly disappeared.

I saw their spaceship leaving
And felt extremely sad,
For I wish I could have told them
Not all of us are bad.

Lucy Bradley (12)
The Lady Eleanor Holles School, Hampton

Be Thankful

Nothing in life is fully appreciated.
Even though when you think about it there are children out there dying
People suffering and ill
Mothers holding their babies crying.

We take things for granted,
Things are always just there;
We never have to worry that much,
We do not really care.

We make a fuss over a sore throat
Or a cold that is going around,
There are children in the Third World, everywhere with illnesses
Looking for cures that have not been found.

Why are we so selfish?
We never stop and think.
Life for us is so easy,
They have to walk miles just to get a drink.

How hard life is for them!
We should be so much more grateful;
There are many charities that we could support,
The people that work for these charities are so faithful.

They believe that we can help these people,
That we can make a difference;
Why don't you think about that?
Help them, make their Christmas.

Avril O'Neill (11)
The Lady Eleanor Holles School, Hampton

Evacuee's Promise

Ribbons of steam and forlorn goodbyes
Interweave in a frantic evacuation tapestry.
The train chugs away as London looks on,
Tattered by bombs.
Carriages cut through the countryside far from war,
Unravelling futures.

A kind family awaits me, with children of their own,
Children I can play with.
Not another family, not the silence from Gerry's bombs -
Home is all I want.

I shall be foul-mouthed,
Slap the children, refuse to eat.
They will be kind.
They will teach me to bake and swim.
But I will spill the flour
And ignore the river as it murmurs its cascade
Of spells.

I will *not* go to school.
The fields will feel my tread upon their backs.
The countryside shall wince in fear as I tear
Branches from trees and laugh as flowers
Cower beneath me.

The family will relent.
They will send me back to the terror-stricken city.
Back to bombs and war.
Back to Mother.
Back to normal.

Elizabeth Donnelly (12)
The Lady Eleanor Holles School, Hampton

School Dinners

Queuing for almost three hundred hours
In line for the most disgusting food
Made with fungi and poisonous flowers
Trying not to throw up, as that would be rude.

One by one, we all enter
Showing our cards to the teacher at the front
Into the revolting food centre
Chips and nuggets is all *we* want.

But no, something healthy and filling
Like worms and maggots too
Come on, try to be willing
If you turn your head sideways, it doesn't look like poo.

Holding out your plates -
A dollop of slime
Trying to stick with all your mates
While trying not to push out of line.

A smile from the dinner ladies
Who are laughing with glee
My food looks like a baby's
Do they think I'm only three?

I stare at the water in my glass
I'm thirsty, but I dare not drink
As I watch the fly swim slowly past
I prod him to try and make him sink.

Pick up my crumble, or is it sawdust?
And my apple looks like it's been kept for years
I don't want to eat it, but I must
I gag as the dinner lady sneers.

Fleur Wheatley (12)
The Lady Eleanor Holles School, Hampton

The Sandwich

It sits there,
It just sits there, quietly,
I know it's watching me
And it knows it'll win,
Eventually.

'Go on,' a little voice whispers,
'You know you want to.'
The smell of warm bread,
The bubbling of melted cheese,
Tempting.

What if I only took a tiny bite?
Would my sister see?
I close my eyes,
Take a step back,
So much self-control.

I can't do it,
The smell forces me forward,
My hand reaches out,
My mouth opens,
Perfection in a mouthful.

It's all gone,
Three big bites,
Nothing left to show,
Apart from several crumbs
And greed.

I feel so bad now,
My sister will find out
And my stomach hurts,
Maybe I'm ill or maybe it's just
Guilt!

Michelle Gomes (14)
The Lady Eleanor Holles School, Hampton

Anything

When told to write on anything,
It's such a task to do.
There are choices upon choices,
But I still don't have a clue.

What subject shall I write about?
How long does it have to be?
Is it best to write in verses,
Or Haiku poetry?

Shall I make my poem rhyme,
Using lots of similes?
Or write it as a limerick?
Should the choice be one of these?

But it's Thursday night already
And time is running out,
What shall I give tomorrow?
What should it be about?

Amber Bissell (12)
The Lady Eleanor Holles School, Hampton

The Winning Run

As I stood at the line
With nothing else on my mind
But to come first in the race
As we started I set my own pace
Finally the finish line was in sight
But that's all
That is in my sight!
As I ran past the finish line
I jumped with excitement
All I could think of
Was that trophy.

Daniel Broadhurst (11)
The Matthew Arnold School, Staines

Summer

Summertime is so much fun,
New green flowers in the sun,
Living life as it should be,
All together, you and me,
Summer dresses, shorts and skirts,
Now nobody's in the lurks,
Summertime, so much fun,
Love and care for everyone,
Soon comes winter in the air,
The wind blusters, do I care?
Snowballs, snowmen, Christmas too,
A time for family, Mum, Dad and you,
Soon the Christmas tree goes up,
Abbie, my sister's up early enough,
Family greets, but soon say goodbye,
Ready for spring, everyone give a sigh,
Spring is here, leaves grow back,
Ready for summer when it attacks!

Amy Willmott (11)
The Matthew Arnold School, Staines

High Mates Trip

High Ashurst was great
Kept playing with mates
We did lots of things
No jewellery, like rings
We had lunch
And some teachers
Had the hump
And a bump
And a scary jump
And I fell off my chair
Showing my underwear!

Limara Hayes (11)
The Matthew Arnold School, Staines

Emotions

Emotions, emotions!
Lots of different kinds
You can find.
Emotions!

Love
Love can be cruel,
Love can be blind.
Love can be lovely,
Love can be all sorts.

Emotions, emotions!
Lots of different kinds
You can find.
Emotions!

Hate
Hate can be physical,
Hate can be mental.
Hate can be verbal,
Hate is *mean.*

Emotions, emotions!
Lots of different kinds,
You can find.
Emotions!

Envy
Envy is green,
Envy is jealousy.
Envy gives you problems,
Envy is bad.

Emotions, emotions!
Lots of different kinds,
You can find.
Emotions!

Happiness
Happiness is good for the heart,
Happiness won't let your heart fall apart.
Happiness can be love,
Happiness feels great!

Emotions!
Emotions!

Nina Athi (12)
The Matthew Arnold School, Staines

Lost

As your children look up at you
You don't see it in their face.
They smile at you to try to see
What they used to see in Grace.

I look at you, Daddy, to see your face
It used to seem so bright.
But when you came back, all cold and grey,
It didn't seem quite right.

The grey of your eyes
Were black with fear
As you laid there still
Throughout the year.

As pale as a ghost
Your dull, white skin
Was stretched so tight
So gaunt, so thin.

The love you cared for
Did disappear
But the love in your heart,
Will soon reappear.

Rebecca Wright (16) & Lucy Cass (15)
The Matthew Arnold School, Staines

The Castle

The castle looks so clean
Cleanliness is forgotten
Forgotten by the people
The people dealing with *death.*

The castle, it whispers
Whispers the secrets
Secrets from the past
The past that is full of *death.*

The castle was full of murderers
The murderers were the disease
Disease that killed the families
The families dealing with *death.*

The news is full of death
Death frightens everybody
Everybody always forgets
Forgets that life is worth
Living.

Cassie Garland (12)
The Matthew Arnold School, Staines

Dogs

Dogs are cool, dogs are fine,
Better than cats or any kind,
Dogs you walk,
Dogs are fine,
Any great dog is a friend of mine,
You could walk with them to Bristol Zoo,
To B&Q,
Back home again for a barbecue!
Give it a drink,
Give it some food,
Dogs are the best!

Shalini Sharma & Jack Shuttleworth (11)
The Matthew Arnold School, Staines

My Grandad

My grandad is fat and cuddly
And he's a lad,
He is very good with electricity
And with wood, he's not so bad,
But when it comes to plumbing,
He sometimes gets mad.

He changed the kitchen sink one day
And thought it would be all right,
But when he turned the taps on,
My mum got a fright!
Water poured onto the ceiling,
Water poured onto the floor,
Water almost went everywhere
And my mum walked out the door!

She did not come back till teatime,
By then she had calmed down,
She thought she'd better come back to see,
If we had drowned!

Bobbie Jo Williams (12)
The Matthew Arnold School, Staines

Michael Owen

M y best goal was against
I reland
C hampions England, 2-1 to us
H aving a bottle of champagne
A fter the game
E ngland loved me after I scored the winning goal
L oving every minute of my England career

O n the ball is Michael Owen
W ith the ball running round the defenders
E ager to score the only goal
N ot even the goalkeeper could save his striking shot, it's a *goal!*

Joshua W Morrish (11)
The Matthew Arnold School, Staines

Cats

Cats are the best,
They're not a pest, only if they want food,
If you say no, they're not in a good mood,
Only if you do what they like.
There's a dog called Spike,
Who chases cats,
But cats also eat rats!
Cats are nice,
They play with dice, if they're in a good mood,
But if they're not,
Cats can scratch and bite!
Cats are cute,
They're not a brute,
Cats are just the best!
I have a cat,
He chases rats,
His name is Oscar.
He is the cutest cat ever!
He is nice,
He eats up mice,
He is the cutest ever cat!

Rosie Irwin (11)
The Matthew Arnold School, Staines

Food

Food, food, wonderful food
No need ever for you to be rude
Eat with knives and forks if you wish
But there's no excuse when it's your favourite dish
Unlimited food, a big buffet
Eat what you want, it's totally okay
You won't be obese, you won't be fat
You'll put on some weight and that is that
Food is great, food is fine
And when you eat some, you're on cloud nine!

Zeyna Zafar (11)
The Matthew Arnold School, Staines

Christmas

Christmas is a time
Of year for happy
Times and times
To cheer.

Christmas is
For everyone
And Christmas
Time has
Just begun.

So come
On in
And join the
Fun, so everyone
Can have some
Fun.

Gemma Zaremba (11)
The Matthew Arnold School, Staines

My High Ashurst Poem

I think High Ashurst is great
Let's pray we're not late.

The archery is brill,
Let's hope we get a thrill.

The high ropes were scary,
Let's just be a little bit wary.

We went on the zip wire,
We went off like a bit of fire.

But then it was time to go
And I was feeling very low.

Peter Mack (11)
The Matthew Arnold School, Staines

High Ashurst

When we went to High Ashurst
We had lots and lots of fun
We did every activity under the sun.

We also did some rock climbing
That was really fun
I'd like to do that again
Because it was so fun, fun!

We also did some teamwork
That was really fun
I'd like to do that again
Because we had to run.

I really enjoyed my day
It was really, really fun
I'd like to go again
With my dad and mum.

Lisa Taylor (11)
The Matthew Arnold School, Staines

Charlie Bray

C haz Mick bimbo
H ave a nice day
A nd a bit confused
R eally weird
L ucky you didn't say banana
I diotic
E mpora . . .

B rainy - *not*
R aving mad
A lunatic
Y ip yap yabalob.

Charlie Bray (11)
The Matthew Arnold School, Staines

My Family

My mum's upstairs, in bed,
My dad is in the back room, watching the rugby,
My sister's playing on the computer.

What am I to do?
I suppose there is my homework,
Even though it is a bore,
I think I'll have a little snooze
On the red settee.

When I woke up I could smell the smell of dinner,
We were having chicken fajitas again,
Yummy, yummy, yummy.

I really love my family,
They are really great,
Thank you for making them great.

Bethan Mansell (11)
The Matthew Arnold School, Staines

Nervously

Nervously the mouse runs from the cat
Nervously the rabbit pops out the hat.

Nervously the baby waits for an injection
Nervously the town runs from the deadly infection.

Nervously the couple share their first kiss
Nervously the warrior gave the battle a miss.

Nervously the elder stands up to a punk
Nervously the fish swims through the black gunk.

But probably the most nervous of all is
Me, on a ride, that's 60 feet tall
That's all!

Alice Ford (12)
The Matthew Arnold School, Staines

Dear Santa

Dear Santa
I've been so good
Well, as good as I could!
There's some things I'd like
Like a brand new bike
Or something cool
Like a swimming pool
Or a cute pet
I could take to the vet
But most of all
Is something small
A great Christmas
To one and all!

Have a great Christmas everyone!

Verity Rose Martin (11)
The Matthew Arnold School, Staines

Shopping

I love shopping, shopping, shopping
There is no stopping, stopping, stopping
It's good to go, go, go
You can't say no, no, no.

You buy a bag, you buy a hat
Might even buy a bed for your cat
You spend your money
It's so, so funny.

I love shopping, shopping, shopping
There is no stopping, stopping, stopping
It's good to go, go, go
You can't say no, no, no!

Demi Girdler & Vikki Stroud (12)
The Matthew Arnold School, Staines

My Pet And His Flea

I had a new pet that I brought into school
All the kids and the teachers thought it was cool.

But I have a problem and a problem it is
My pet had a flea that no one could miss.

The flea on my pet grew ever so tall
So I got sent out of class by Mr Dall.

He marched up and down shouting at me
But it wasn't my fault, it was the flea!

I called for my pet, it could not be seen
I heard a shout from English, it's Mr McBean!

Oh no! Oh dear! I'm dead, I'm dead
And out came McBean with the flea on his head!

But where's my Fluffy, Fluffy my pet
Sorry old chum, he's squashed and he's dead.

I cried and I cried, I cried out loud
The flea stepped down and looked and he bowed.

So I have a new pet and it is a flea
We play in the park and sail out to sea.

Sam Yates (12)
The Matthew Arnold School, Staines

Food, Food

Food, food is very tasty
Food, food is very delicious
Food, food is like us but different
Food, food is very good when you are hungry
Food, food is very good for my tummy and it is very yummy
Food, food is very healthy for you.

Lauren Loveridge
The Matthew Arnold School, Staines

School Morning Rap

I got up in the morning
Brushed my hair
In front of me
The clothes I gotta wear.

Packed my bags
Brush my teeth
Look in the mirror
There's last night's beef.

I'm out on the road
Saw a cat
Oh my God
He looks so fat.

A car passes by
A mate inside
Exhaust so black
Smells like someone died!

There are the gates
Bold and green
There is a teacher
He looks so mean.

Jordan Phillips (11)
The Matthew Arnold School, Staines

The Boneyard Rap

This is the rhythm of the boneyard rap,
Make your heart beat as fast as you can,
Make your hair fuzzy, dark and black,
Put on the music which is rock and roll,
When the people walk in the cemetery
Scare them, scare them,
Till they're *sick!*

Jaime Amanda Rhodes (11)
The Matthew Arnold School, Staines

My High Ashurst Poem

Today is the day I go on a school trip,
When I get there I would love to try rock climbing but I need a grip.
Now it's the coach ride to the High Ashurst park,
I've heard there are woods there and they're very dark.
Finally we get there,
There's a big rock climbing wall, all I've done is stare.
We have to line up in our groups, we've got an instructor, James,
Now we're doing the challenge course, it looks like some games.
Next is rock climbing, have to work as a team,
It's not that hard as it's meant to seem.
Now is high ropes climbing,
Of the milk crate building.
Off to the leap of faith, time to jump, 1, 2, 3!
Two of my friends and me.
It's been a long day,
Time to go away.
This moment is here to keep,
I'm so tired, I think I might have a sleep
On the coach.

Stephen Dean (11)
The Matthew Arnold School, Staines

Colour Poem

Blue is the colour of the sea
It is the colour I see
Blue is the colour of the sky
It makes me want to fly
Blue is a cold colour
It makes you feel so bold
Blue is the colour of sad
It makes me glad
Blue is the colour of water
It is a slaughter.

Shaun Parr (11)
The Matthew Arnold School, Staines

I Like Noise

I like noise
The drum goes *bang!* The guitar goes *twang!*
My baby brother *giggles!*
The piano goes *ping!* The bells go *ding!*
I love my imaginary band.
My dad's shed is *revving!*
The bike is *thundering!*
My dad is working again
The kitchen is *popping!*
I can hear the *chopping!*
My mum is cooking our tea
In my bar, laughing and fighting
And noises I don't always know.
My house, my home
Is one big noise
And without it I'd feel on my own.
I love noise.

Samule Thornton (11)
The Matthew Arnold School, Staines

High Ashurst

H igh Ashurst
I s excellent
G reat
H igh

A chievements
S tunning
H ard work
U nusual
R espect
S trange
T rust.

Jake O'Leary (11)
The Matthew Arnold School, Staines

Food Is Great

The future is fat mama, eating all the wrong fat foods, yeah!
You should be paying off debts, not buying cigarettes
Everybody needs food, everybody needs to chew
Everybody needs to eat, eat, eat
But you should eat healthy food not just sweets
And all that fatty junk
But everybody should stop and think
What am I going to eat today?
Not yesterday's food, but five portions of fruit
Like oranges and apples, bananas and strawberries
And vegetables are great for you too.
They are well balanced and have a great taste
But everybody should go with what they want
That's how life should be, should be.

Sarah Weller (12)
The Matthew Arnold School, Staines

Me

My mum is knitting jumpers
My dad's fallen asleep
My gran's out playing bingo
She sometimes wins a streak.

My grandad's at the allotment
Although it's bound to rain
My sister's playing Beyoncé
Over and over again.

What a lovely family
What a lovely lot
Sometimes we're together
And sometimes we're not.

Ellimay Macmillan (11)
The Matthew Arnold School, Staines

My Dog

My dog is jet black
He has a red toy
His name is Jack
He is a boy.
He doesn't like other dogs
He likes to sleep
He sits on logs
He likes to leap.
He eats like a pig
He likes his belly tickled
I dress him up in wigs
When he walks, he wiggles.
He's very soft and cuddly
He's always lively and bubbly.

Emma Roome (14)
The Matthew Arnold School, Staines

Sport

Sport, sport, sport!
When I do swimming,
I am always winning.
I know a punk
And he can do a slam dunk.
When I play football and do a strike,
I am as fast as a pike.
When I play cricket,
I hit the wicket.
I am cunning,
When I do running.
Sport is always fun,
When you have a starting gun.

James Porter (12)
The Matthew Arnold School, Staines

Friendship Poem

Take your faithful spoon
Then you are ready to do your mix
It should be ready in two ticks
First you put 200g of trust
And mix it well
Or he will smell
Then add 1tsp of common interest
And he will be the best
Then you stir so there's no bumps
Or lumps
Add 3 litres of funny
And he will be a happy bunny
Add 4 cups of feelings
So he's not revealing
Then add sprinkles of awareness
So he's not careless
Then 10 kilograms of strength
And this will go a big length
Then 10 kilograms of kindness
So he's not spineless
And 200g of honesty
Then 5 pints of understanding
So he's not so demanding.

When it's done, you'll be glad
Because he will be the best friend you've ever had.

Charles Berry (11)
The Matthew Arnold School, Staines

Live Forever

(Inspired by 'Do Not Stand At My Grave And Weep' by Mary Frye and Wilbur Skeels)

Do not stand by my tomb and cry,
I am not there, I did not die.
I went with honour, went with pride,
Pushed all the fear and doubt inside.

I marched out there and stood up tall,
I did not stumble, would not fall.
You weep for me now, but you will see,
Just leave me here and let it be.

For I am happy I went away,
I am happy I fought that day.
I fought for my country and for our freedom
And through it all, I found a reason.

A reason to be there, a reason to fight,
With all my strength and with all my might.
I did not go and fight in vain,
I did not suffer, I felt no pain.

It gave me freedom, it let me live,
I know I gave all I had to give.
I've gone to Heaven to live above
And look down upon the ones I love.

I will no longer walk along the battlefield,
My soul is immortal, even though I was killed.
For I am a martyr, I am a saint,
Memories of me will never be faint.

I'll be with you in your heart
And so we can never be apart.
Do not stand by my tomb and cry,
I am not there, I did not die.

Lana Wright (15)
The Matthew Arnold School, Staines

Colours

R ead my lips as I speak my words
E ncourage your friend to not break a boy's heart
D efinite yes to a question you ask

B lank out your old thoughts and put new ones in
L ive your life as if you were king
U se your thoughts to pass you by and you'll
E nd up with a bright blue sky

G raceful colours everywhere
R ound the world you cannot stare
E verywhere green lies
E ven in the blue skies
N obody can escape from green.

Gemma Constant (12)
The Matthew Arnold School, Staines

High Ashurst Poem

H igh Ashurst is good, better than I thought it was
I t was great and I wasn't late
G reat time I had, let's go again with chocolate and ice cream
H igh Ashurst is the best, better than the rest

A s we came to the ropes it was fun and it shot down like a gun
S winging about on the trampeze was a little scary but really fun
H igh Ashurst, yeah, I would love to go again
U p, down on zip wire and really fast too
R unning everywhere, so excited, you don't know where to start
S tarting at the ropes was really good, we didn't need coats
T ime to go home, love to go again.

Jade Crespo (11)
The Matthew Arnold School, Staines

High Ashurst

H is for high ropes
I is for impressive
G is for great
H is for harness

A is for activities
S is for surprising activities
H is for hard hats
U is for an unusual experience
R is for rock climbing
S is for stacking crates
T is for teamwork.

Adele Langley (11)
The Matthew Arnold School, Staines

Autumn

(Inspired by one reading of Keats' 'To Autumn')

Season of exhaust fumes and mild fruitfulness,
Close bosom-friend of the advancing sun:
Scheming with him to load and bless,
The ground littered with beer cans,
With a sweet scent; and still more,
Later flowers for the pests,
Until they think warm days will never cease,
For summer has o'er brimmed their clammy cells.

Who hath heard the birds above the drone of the aeroplanes?
Drowsed with the fume of engines,
Who here can hear the natural songs of autumn? Aye, where are they?
Think not of them, thou hast thy music too -
The angry shouts of the horn,
The scream of an upset child and that of her mother.
Oh yes, thou hearest nature here,
The bang of the conker against the window of a car.
The crunch of leaves against the concrete,
The man-made in contrast with that of nature.

Ann Wiltshire (16)
Twyford CE High School, Acton

Like Autumn

My love, you're like the Autumn - golden bliss.
And in every dewy leaf I see your face.
Breezy winds caress, as if to kiss,
And gently whisper that they know my place.
It's next to you, your hazel hair so close,
And on a bed of dying leaves we lie.
But you blossom from the dying like a rose,
As together, we gaze at the slowly-moving sky.

Then,

I wake up, beside a crooked tree, alone.
On all, a silent mask of dreamy sorrow.
The branches by my side your empty throne,
My dreams ignored, at least until Tomorrow.

The sun is out, but the moon can still be seen,
Hoping to steal Autumn with pale lies.
With icy claws he takes you for his Queen,
Because Autumn is captured and tamed inside your eyes.

But,

You hardly ever speak to me,
Except to say, 'Hello,'
And I'm last on your list,
But I care for you the most.
So unfair,
That when our eyes meet;
I have to look away,
Not brave enough to tell you,
That you've turned my heart to clay.

If you knew the truth, the winds would gently say,
'This is your place, right here, beside this boy.'
And I'd be with you, for evermore to stay,
With the woman that I love,
My Autumn Joy.

Adam Wynne (16)
Twyford CE High School, Acton

To Autumn

(Inspired by one reading of Keats' 'To Autumn')

Season of leaves mingling amongst harsh concrete;
Huddles of students clad thickly in scarves,
Graffiti littering a lone bench seat;
And the guiding streetlamps comfort dusk paths.
Determined rain that breaks at your door;
With wind muffled by the distant traffic throb
Luke-warm weather stubbornly in-between;
And delayed trains that utter a stifled sob.
Forsaking birds shun their nests - away they soar,
Flowers have deserted, crumpled to the floor,
Our mouths produce mists of a hazy sheen.

As cold ambles in, we wrap ourselves in sleep,
Not wanting to embrace the tired town
Tea is downed, so heat through our veins does seep
And we dress in murky grey, blue or brown.
Yet colour is displayed in the twilight sky
Or in the ghost orange of Hallowe'en.
Old cigarette smell laces in the air
Whilst the buskers practice a lullaby.
But now the grass is deliciously green
In the parks, a haven space for the serene,
Though night screams the sound of a firework flare.

The time fleets past, a place of hurried change
Unlike summer, who breathes her days long.
But I would rather a thousand fall days
For that is where my London does belong.
Where coarse nature and humanity meet,
Trees scraping softly the houses of brick
Living hedges decorate a new road
Without nature, the city is not complete.
These things signify that we have not lost,
The nature of autumn, we still have her trust
And she is welcome in her urban abode.

Sarah Ashman (16)
Twyford CE High School, Acton

To Autumn

(Inspired by one reading of Keats' 'To Autumn')

Season of fog and rainy gloominess!
Sending blanket clouds to steal away the sun;
Conspiring with the wind how to cheat our scarves
And touch the spine, where shivers like insects run;
To bend our backs to strive against malicious breeze,
Making hope, like leaves, fall to the floor;
As night envelops day, we rise in dim twilight
The birds' joke: what animal rises before dawn?
To pack themselves into metal machines
And battle through the rushing leaves,
To toil away the hours, in the dusty half-night.

Who hath not seen thee carpeting the ground?
Beneath the wrecks of once proud canopies
Colours of forgotten sun, showered all around,
As squirrels, silent, stand at ease;
Then leap to business, storing spring,
So they may rest and sleep in peace
Dream 'til first light enters their musty home
Their wake-up call the choir of bees,
Who raise their voice as one and sing
Saluting their returning king
Once more upon his radiant throne.

Where are the songs of spring? Where are they now?
Sounding so distant, a half-remembered tune;
Our season's music cannot sing loud,
Outdone by the roaring of the fumes
Which feed the barren wastes of white
That hang above, a ceiling snow,
In which the birds can shriek and fly
And soar above on wings as light
As leaves and laugh at those below
Who cannot follow where they go;
Above the autumn, in the sky.

Jamie Hitch (16)
Twyford CE High School, Acton

Venture

(Inspired by 'The Send Off' by Wilfred Owen)

Excited, the adventure starts,
A buzz as energy attacks each man.
Laughter, banter and play,
As the track enters the misty horizons beyond the station.

The men line up, all tall and proud,
In their crisp, new uniforms.
Handsome, young and strong,
New polished boots,
Shiny as their girlfriend's new ring.

Everyone is privileged but sad,
A tear fallen beneath the girlfriend.
The mother weeps
And the daughter dreams to fight for her country one day.
A trail of smoke is left, as the soldiers leave their old lives behind.

They left like idols leaving a stage,
Creating a ripple effect on loved ones,
Of sadness and honour.
Their fate is uncertain,
But their adventure is clear.

He wonders,
As he fingers the locket and photos.
Of course, he would never forget her,
After all, he would be back for Christmas.

He will see his beautiful son.
Will there be cheers, high spirits and dancing?
A party, perhaps?
Arrival, in the dark night,
The son is asleep
And there is no party.
For the village is injured.

Esmé Osborne (15)
Twyford CE High School, Acton

War Time

(Inspired by 'The Send Off' by Wilfred Owen)

Stepping into the endless, darkening platform
Soldiers innocently leaving the trail
Of echoed footsteps behind.

Helmets carelessly strapped on,
Yet ideal for camouflage: dirty and greener than envy
The outfit: clearly approachable and taken pride in, to put on
The true lie hidden deep within each one's doubts.

The mother hopelessly takes a close observation
To what could be her final look at her 'still' youthful son
Toddlers weep, wail at a father they barely know
Too innocent are they to understand
Slowly but surely, does the black carriage snatch away:
Sons, husbands, fathers.

On a serious ride to a destination
Which they are foreign to and
Brave are they to be leaving, like they will witness
Their children grow.

The memories of the 'goodbyes' remembered:
'Promise me you'll be back soon.'
He promised to, of course,
Knowing that a lie is being told.

A triumphant win, the nation cheering
A triumphant achievement returning home safely
But, no: only a legless soldier,
With wounds which are unable to heal.
A father which has been replaced
And memories of death that wipe away a hero's moral.

Grace Ho (15)
Twyford CE High School, Acton

Off To War

(Inspired by 'The Send Off' by Wilfred Owen)

In the car on the way to the station, with fields flashing past the
window,
Possibly for the last time because it's off to war they go,
The station, milling with families and the nerves are beginning to show.

Dressed in their immaculate uniforms,
Their brass buttons twinkling in the early morning glow,
Like their children's faces that glisten with tears that flow.

Everyone has come to see their people go,
Beloved fathers, sons and brothers,
The air is filled with weeping lovers and mothers,
As the great beast chugs out into the dawning day.

They left like royalty, with their adoring crowds surrounding them,
All of this for a few unknown men,
But where would the train lead them?
They knew not.

The tears flowed down the faces of wives and lovers,
A rose in their hands to signify their love,
'I love you,' whispered from trembling lips.

The station milling with loved ones,
Would their lover be on the train?
Best Sunday clothes are worn,
To herald the triumphant return of the soldiers.
The home is now filled with the gurgles of a baby,
Will everything return to normal?
Maybe, just maybe.

Helen McBride (15)
Twyford CE High School, Acton

A War Poem

(Inspired by 'The Send Off' by Wilfred Owen)

Marching to the beat, they travel to the station,
No one knowing what to expect,
All is silent as they wait for the train.

Standing in line, waiting, all dressed the same,
All as silent as the dead,
Like a sea of green.

As they step on the train, passers-by stop,
They wave at them, with smiles on their faces,
As the train departs, some shout and some cheer,
Though this fades as the train pulls away,
Carrying them to the uncertain.

They left like heroes, smiling and waving,
Leaving to save us all,
Though behind the cheer, the uncertainty is clear.

The voices still echo in their heads,
'Come back to me, come back soon,'
The mud and the blood, soak through those proud uniforms,
As they dream of returning home.

Arriving home, he opens the door,
'I'm home, I'm home, I'm home at last,'
But to have to go back, can he deal with the horror?
To face that experience again?
After returning to a home which he took so for granted,
A home that will never be the same.

Sarah Winterburn (15)
Twyford CE High School, Acton

Embrace

(Inspired by 'The Send Off' by Wilfred Owen)

The group of curious, freshly-clothed men
Walked towards the start of their adventure
A cold and frosty morning, where every breath, froze their hearts.

The group of dirty mud jumpers and khaki green trousers
Crackled with every step, like the first frost of winter
They appeared to be strong, courageous men, with their
Backpacks full to the brim and metal-toed shoes
They were like autumn leaves, just fallen the newcomers
                    of the death march.

The group of lovers, fathers, uncles and grandfathers,
                    choked from their tears
A brave wave from each hand, receiving the blessings of their families
A little boy dressed in his best jacket, ran to his father
                    for one last embrace
'I want to grow up to be like you, Daddy,' he whimpers
The departing train enveloped the men
Like a mother to her children.

The group of uncertain fighters left like the colourful sunset in the sky
Each thought of each soldier had a different, yet vivid colour
Together these colours mixed into a murky, brown cloud
Which lingered above them, similar to their uncertainty
                    of their destination.

The group of homesick souls, queried about their return
None of them knew if they would ever see their beloved families again
The soldiers' lovers cling onto their hopes and prayers;
'You will return, you will succeed, I will be waiting for you.'

The group of high-hoped heroes, excited for their return
Imagine feasts of exquisite food and ale
A warm, cosy house, with a warm, cosy reception
Will their families remember them?
Their lovers still love them?
The harsh wind's in their faces, so piercing, so harsh, eyes weep

Eager spirits of praise and glory
Minds running riot
Home could be the end of the war for their souls
Or maybe, more vicious than a knife in their souls
Could this be their last embrace?

Abby Pilkington (16)
Twyford CE High School, Acton

In Autumn
(Inspired by one reading of Keats' 'To Autumn')

Season of footprints and smoky breath
Of children drawing on frosted glass
Naked trees approaching death
The crunching of feet upon icy grass
Greys and blues litter the sky
Explosions of colour from dull, metal bars
The shortened days go drifting by
Autumn has again begun
Through biting wind, with blinding sun
And the dreaded splash from passing cars.

Rebekah Read (16)
Twyford CE High School, Acton

To Autumn
(Inspired by one reading of Keats' 'To Autumn')

The time has arrived, with the fresh autumnal breeze,
A fading sun, ever present,
With the warm coloured leaves, scattered amongst the floor
Sweet and fair twittering of the birds, pierced by roaring engine.
Everlasting sounds of the busy streets, awaken the early mornings,
My hair soft lifted by the winnowing wind,
To autumn, a season of fresh air.

Ali Mirza (16)
Twyford CE High School, Acton

Autumn

(Inspired by one reading of Keats' 'To Autumn')

Seasons of fog and brightened skies,
Embrace of mist and harsh air
Conspiring with the piercing noises of civilisation
Car alarms; alerts to those who care
The cries of a child carried through bitter silence
To ears of those with misty eyes
Grey walls, grey doors, grey skies, grey lives
Stars concealed by deceiving light
Looming blocks of human hives
Everlasting grey twilight, streaked with green
Of ever-dwindling beauty left to fight.
The red has come to join the grey
And merge as one unholy sight
Dying reminders of what has been.

Carcasses of leaves that were
Lie in unassuming wait for prey
Who step upon their darkening spine
And slip into the sheet of grey.
The scent of damp encircles the streets
Creatures hide in fear for long months
Emerging once the sun can again shine
Rain bringing hail, bringing snow, bringing sleet
It is the warning of the next in line
The dark, the cold, the damp, the death
Leading to winter's long-awaited retreat.

Hannah Jane Wright (16)
Twyford CE High School, Acton

The Long-Awaited Departure

(Inspired by 'The Send Off' by Wilfred Owen)

Slowly, sleepy soldiers emerged onto the darkening platform.
A sickening stench filled the misty air,
As brave boys nervously awaited their orders.

In their freshly pressed uniforms, they stood,
Stiff, with their faces hidden beneath a fearful stare,
Like naughty children about to be severely punished.

Mothers painfully watched,
As their sons were soon to be snatched away into the night.
The train waited anxiously for its saddened soldiers to finally board,
Tired, it would carry its passengers to their new military stations.
Forced to say goodbye, soldiers hugged their frightened relations.

As the sun departed, the cold of the darkness swept over us,
As the train silently steamed off into the distance, fading from our sight
Like precious jewels stolen from our grasp,
Into an unknown territory.

The uncertainty of their return had been burning thoughts,
Grieving consequences that some may have to face.
Realities that were not to be dwelt on.

Hopefully, they would be heroes, returning to a glorious welcome.
But what if this was not the case?
Would they return, greeted with silence?
Broken, changed men, escaping brutality, eyes were made to see,
Regretful of the *brave* men they were forced to be.

Slowly, sleepy soldiers will emerge onto a darkening platform.

Rozinder Kaur Gill (15)
Twyford CE High School, Acton

Ready?

(Inspired by 'The Send Off' by Wilfred Owen)

It's cold - but not inside us,
With fire burning through our hearts,
we're ready to fight as heroes, we're ready.

Dull, green swarms, moving together:
Heavy boots, warm jackets, hard hats all
In time, together. The train appears, we're ready.

All around the smiling faces, crying with pride and longing,
They all have to laugh, at the soldiers' flat singing.
The train, it halts, it jolts, it stops,
Large carriages in all their glory. The rain, it drops
But is left unnoticed. They're ready, the men, we're ready.

Left as lions, strong and brave.
When they return, they will be - be heroes
They were ready.

They said it was easy, they will return
They will be fighting, killing, they should return.
I hope they are ready, I love you, return.

I wished it would be the same, but everyone wasn't.
I was to be a hero, a lion, brave - so friends thought,
But this way was not for glory, just death, slaughter.
Why did we leave in the beginning, all lies?
We were not prepared. We were not ready.

Catherine Duckmanton (15)
Twyford CE High School, Acton

Mother's Pride

(Inspired by 'The Send Off' by Wilfred Owen)

My mother straightened out my collar
'How grand you look,' she said
I felt so privileged and excited
I was going to war
Taking my last glance at my house
I saw my mother wave
I was going to make her proud.

The train station was a sea of happy faces
Hustling and bustling
Soldiers parted from their families
United, we boarded the train
We stood, strong and proud
Yet, questions nagged my mind
Where were we going?
Would I be missed?
Would I return?

I survived
But aged by the horrors of war
The station was filled with anxiety
Mothers searched desperately
The knocker whimpered and my mother appeared
She was terribly thin.

Lydia Bothamley (15)
Twyford CE High School, Acton

Celebrations Of Bravery

(Inspired by 'The Send Off' by Wilfred Owen)

As evening fell, a group of boys, young, pure of thought,
March manfully to the train platform,
With hope of glory, triumph and honour,
Yet untouched by the clamour of war.

Boys though, dressed in newly starched uniforms,
Like newborn lambs to their fate.

Distant eyes gaze from dark corners,
Stray dogs scavenge for food,
As they are herded into the waiting train.

They left like magic,
Once there, then gone,
To arrive at some uncertain destination.

Thick in doubt, lovers wait for news,
A letter, a poem, or worse, most feared,
A knock at the door.

But if they returned, what would they meet?
No heroic welcome, or celebrations of bravery.
And how would it feel to know that you're home
Packed with speeches of conflict and courage,
With nobody there to listen?
Too few to draw a crowd.

Mica Lloyd (15)
Twyford CE High School, Acton

One Fine Day

I see them float through the waking morning air,
The filth-trodden leaves beneath them
As they ascend onto the carriage,
They must have souls as pure as fresh snow, hearts encased in gold.

They wear the faces of eager cubs upon a first mission to tackle prey
Their eyes are gleaming lanterns in dark and unprepared faces.
I see them carry the hard back, the strong thigh
And the deep dimple rooted in a soft, red cheek.

The train's ready to depart and smoke drifts across their brave faces,
I know they leave behind joyous families, mothers too proud to turn
up?
The wives emerging from the corners run towards them
Their tears make faint prints in the dirt
And suddenly, all around me happiness and high spirits are lost,
How can grief and pain be so contagious on this wonderful day?

And in the distance I now try to find the mist that is the train
But still I hear it choking down the tracks,
Out of sight, not out of mind.

Don't cry, Mrs Jones, it's only for a time,
Soon our victorious soldiers will arrive on our streets paved with gold
And celestial voices will resound in the air,
'You've made it, you've made it, you've made it to victory!'

Cherish Shirley (15)
Twyford CE High School, Acton

A War Poem

(Inspired by 'The Send Off' by Wilfred Owen)

Clock ticking they arrived at the station,
Openly brave, but mentally like a child.
Secretly scared to support our nation.

The vigorous boots, the emblematic uniform,
Disguises their guilt of being too afraid.
They felt as glorious as a summer's day.

Those who watched, sobbed silently into their aprons,
Mostly mothers missing their sons.
'A difficult time for all, y'know,' spoke a soldier,
Tears in his eyes.
Their noble carriage puffed and its breath took them away.

Amongst complete confusion the soldiers led the way.
They led the way to victory, strong and proud.
Not a finger trembled from our sons.

Reassurance from their loved ones held their hope,
Words of everlasting joy and warmth kept them alive,
In pure dream of returning home.

Is home everlasting,
Or are they forgotten?
Questioned uneasy heroes journeying to their real challenge.

Hannah Middleton (15)
Twyford CE High School, Acton

Action Of The Beginning Of War

(Inspired by 'The Send Off' by Wilfred Owen)

It's the morning that all soldiers leave for war.
Travelling there, my thoughts are sore.
The atmosphere is tense, the wind blows soft.

The soldiers' hats cover their identity
Dark green uniforms, it's all so military.

Families waiting for our departure.
Women hugging their sons and dear loved ones,
Shouts of love and encouragement, whistled through the air
The eyes of the train shut, last tears were shed.

No parents wanted to let their babies go;
Some were just sixteen,
How will I know if they will reach safely?

Would it be an early grave for many of us?
The words of my wife, I kept close to me.

When I return, *if* I return
I will always remember my great effort
For this country.
No one knows the time or day of our return.
Will things have changed? Have we made a change?

Jade Champagnie-McKenzie (15)
Twyford CE High School, Acton

Road To The Trenches

(Inspired by 'The Send Off' by Wilfred Owen)

A sea of fresh faces, filled with a buzz
Standing on lies and false glory
Looking around, you'd feel really sad
Their parents will be sorry.

Covered in green, a sign of health
And energy and youth
If only they knew what lay ahead
But they were never told the truth.

Families watch, standing tall and proud
As their heroes disappear in the crowd
Waving goodbye to the big, red train
Unknown to them, it leads to pain.

The train left with a smirk upon its face
Taking the soldiers to a horrifying place
Never to see their loved ones again
On the way to meet their end.

What they've been told, doesn't give them a clue
They think they will be heroes too
The truth is, that they will never return
But sit on the mantelpiece, in a decorative urn.

Martha Handousa (16)
Twyford CE High School, Acton

Autumn

(Inspired by one reading of Keats' 'To Autumn')

Concrete sealed by a musk of decaying orange-brown
The last of the oranges to ripen
Branches shout their morning sounds
The morning rush conceals them
Pupils blinded by the black light
Recoil in numb fear
Senses, steps behind in my muddy tread
My mind warm past summer's clear
Wool, the last resistance against the cold war's fight
Dawn brings her noise with birds' flight
The wakening I had anticipated.

Bobbing heads dressed in synthetic greens and browns
Forceful breaths the last some may send
Sardines in a common room
Uttering warm notes given
Scratching pens painting they write
The final kill near
To their havens a sanctuary from light
Watch Earl Grey's breath sear
Autumn come, my favourite time of year.

Felix Daniel (16)
Twyford CE High School, Acton

The Great Mind Of J R R Tolkien

(A tribute poem on 'The Lord Of The Rings)

Here is a poem about a book,
One that I hold dear.
It simply is a masterpiece,
I read it every year.

The plot as thick as lumpy stew,
The wit - bright as the sun.
The words woven like a work of art,
The storyline full of fun.

The elves are full of magic,
The dwarves are hard as stone.
The men who are ever trembling,
From the dark lord on his throne.

The wizards full of knowledge,
The hobbits with big feet.
The Ents, the massive tree creatures
And the Orcs, I wouldn't want to meet!

There are poems and riddles each chapter
And plenty a-song and rhyme.
Though as there are one thousand pages,
Reading it takes some time!

There's Aragorn the ranger and King,
Elendil's true heir to the throne.
With Narcil - the blade that was broken,
Courageously he fights alone.

Frodo the gentle, young hobbit,
Who bears the ring to its end.
Continuously tormented by Nazgûl,
Driving him right round the bend!

Gandalf the wise old wizard,
Fighting with Anduril by his side.
Into Moria he fell as the Grey
And became White at the turn of the tide.

Smeagol the crafty river-hobbit,
Who should have been locked behind bars.
With Gollum his evil other-self,
Whispering, 'It's ours. The precious is ours!'

That's just a few of the characters,
There's over one hundred I fear.
It will always be my favourite book,
I look forward to reading it next year!

William Lee Rowley (13)
Vyners School, Uxbridge

Great Minds

Great minds always think alike,
Some people like to say.
But normally they are on their own,
When finding the right way.

Take Brunel as an example,
An engineer ahead of his day.
While everyone followed the same path,
He chose a different way.

Now look at Galileo,
He was one who thought twice.
Disagreeing with the powerful church,
He almost paid the price.

Then there's Sir Isaac Newton,
An apple on his head.
Defined the laws of motion,
By which all things are led.

And don't forget Charles Darwin,
Who worked out evolution.
When people back home all found out,
It was a revelation.

These great minds are just some,
Of those who went before.
To show us things another way,
Of that you can be sure.

James Owen (12)
Vyners School, Uxbridge

London

Dark smoke rises over the jagged skyline,
Like the shadows of forever-lost souls,
Intermingling with the crisp, clear air,
Intoxicating it with its poison.

Where a thousand different tongues,
Illuminate the streets with diversity,
An endless river of faces,
Lost beyond vision in a moment.

A city of eternal contrast,
Where a beggar in the gutter,
Can share his path,
With a man rich beyond desire.

Where joy and terror,
Can run in the same street,
Only to be knocked down,
By the ceaseless traffic.

But where my spirit lies.

Sophie Bell (14)
Walthamstow School for Girls, London

Love - The Sick Rose

Have you ever loved someone
But know he didn't care?
Have you ever felt like crying
But know it wouldn't get you anywhere?
Have you ever looked into his eyes
And said a little prayer?
Have you ever looked into his heart
And wished you were there?
Have you ever watched him walking
Not wanting him to go
And whispered, 'I love you'
But never let him know?
Do you cry in the night
And nearly go insane?
There is nothing in the world
That would cause anymore pain.
If I could choose between love and death
I think I'd rather die
Love is fun but hurts so much
And the price you pay is way too high.

Zonaira Tahir (14)
Walthamstow School for Girls, London

A Pencil Set

He gave her a pencil set,
So she wouldn't forget.
She breathes, she doesn't understand.
She looks up when he raises his hand.
Their love is strange,
The set neatly arranged.
Together they draw,
Together they saw.
The picture gleaming,
Her tears streaming.
They draw and change,
This picture so strange.
A river of time,
The soft bell chime.
This picture they drew,
The sword pierced and slew.
The happiness and sorrow,
The colours hollow,
He gave her a pencil set,
So she'd never forget,
His love.

Cathy Kwan (13)
Walthamstow School for Girls, London

Darkness

The night has a thousand eyes,
The day, only one.

The darkness makes it eerie,
The light makes it safe.

A world full of humans, humans full of secrets,
Secrets full of darkness, darkness full of danger.

Witches, vampires, werewolves,
Hunters, fighters, healers.

Humans, animals, plants,
Eaters, growers, dyers.

A world full of strangers, strangers full of life,
Life full of darkness, darkness full of mystery.

The night of darkness, the wonders of danger,
The darkness is cold, the darkness is ice.

You fight for freedom, you die of pain,
You cry of hunger, you sleep forever.

Your mind has a corner, a corner with a secret,
A secret full of darkness, darkness full of nightmares.

The darkness is cold, the darkness is ice,
The darkness is dangerous, the darkness is mysterious.

The darkness is night, the darkness is life,
The darkness is scary, that darkness is you!

Rubina Ali (13)
Walthamstow School for Girls, London

That's How They Perceive Me

As soon as they see me,
That's how they perceive me,
A bully, a thief, a liar
And if that's how they perceive me,
Even before I'm given a chance,
How can my heart now be set on fire?
You don't know, know what it's like to be me,
You don't know what goes on in my mind,
A dozen emotions all clog up inside me,
Asking questions to answers I can't find,
So what, I look different!
So do you!
I don't give you dirty looks though
And point at you!
I know it's wrong, it's not her fault,
But I want attention so I'll turn to assault,
That way, I can tell my side of the story
And someone will take pity upon me,
But it's not pity I want,
It's a chance to be me,
'Cause at the end of the day,
I don't want to be a bully,
But as soon as they see me,
That's how they perceive me,
So if that's how they perceive me,
I don't have a chance to be just . . . me.

Agnes Kamara (12)
Walthamstow School for Girls, London

The Sick Rose

I remember when I found you,
In the dying garden of my life,
You stood out from the barren waste,
The only beauty that had ever grown
And I picked you for myself,
To share with no one else.

I remember when you blossomed,
You filled the empty space,
You showed me dreams and wonder
And I marvelled at your greatness,
The sweetness of your smell,
Your red of red temptation.

I remember when you fell,
In slow motion it seemed,
Each perfect petal smashing to the ground,
I tried to pick you up, to help you,
But your proud thorns,
Made me bleed your redness.

I remember when you faded,
Your beauty drifting in and out of sight,
You could not make me bleed,
Yet you could not make me smile,
Too far to see, to smell, to touch,
I could not get you back.

I remember when you left me,
Each petal falling through the air,
Landing in my heart,
Black and withered, but in my mind
They are the remnants of a shattered memory
That I will keep for evermore.

Hannah Taylor-Young (13)
Walthamstow School for Girls, London

My Love For You

My love for you,
Once did soar,
Alas,
I do not have anymore.

My love for you,
Was fair as a rose,
Alas,
For zooming past it goes.

My love for you,
Was once true,
Alas,
It is now cold, like you.

My love for you,
Did all but fly,
Alas,
There it goes, fluttering by.

My love for you,
Did never fail,
Alas,
You hit me hard, betrayal.

My love for you,
Was firm and good,
Alas,
For do all you would,
My love for you,
At once did fall,
Alas,
Now I have none, not a sliver, none at all.

Carel Bennett Calaguas (14)
Walthamstow School for Girls, London

How Can You Expect Love?

As you stare at me the way you do
You intimidate me and I feel so small
As small as a garden spider
My heart is like an ant, easily crushed
My words have become powerless
Your words are like a thousand stabbing knives
And I'm all alone in this room
But surrounded by enemies and demons
The Devil's work has paid off
His power is working on me, but I'll never give in
I won't let Him win, I won't give Him the satisfaction.

Your stare is pure evil, pure deceit, I can feel it
And in your eyes I can see the evil that consumes you
I can see you as a child, you didn't know any better
But I still have the right to blame you, you hurt me
You disappointed me, how can you expect love from me?
Where will it come from if not from my heart?
Who will you ask why I hate you, if you refuse to listen to my words?
Who are you going to turn to for answers when there's no one left
                                        but you and I?
You made me hard, you made me cold, you made me cry each night
You ripped me apart, how can you expect love in return?
Your eyes and your actions are what told me you work for the Devil.

The sweet scent of pain, the strong essence of hatred and emptiness
The rich taste of revenge, of justice being served
But in your eyes I'm a mistake, the biggest one you made
You can't get rid of me though, my spirit will always remain
And yet you still can't see everything you put me through
I can't remember when it was good, I can't remember a day I smiled
The pain you cause is so intense and strikes so deep
But if I want the end to come I have to bring it forth.

Louisa Spence (14)
Walthamstow School for Girls, London

The Sick Rose

The rose was given to me before he left,
He pressed it into my hands as the tears rolled down his face,
Its thorns dug into my palm as I clasped it tight,
I would let go,
I would not let him leave,
Leave to die,
Like so many before him.

The rose was so fragile,
So delicate,
It could not live long,
But in my grief I would not let it die.

Its petals weakened,
Its colour faded,
Its stem hung,
Withered and old,
I would savour each petal as they fell,
Till they crumbled in my grasp.

When I was told I could not believe, would not believe,
It had been my fault,
I had let the rose die so many months before,
So as the rose before . . .

My petals weakened
My colour faded,
I hung,
Withered and old,
No one there to savour each petal as they fell,
Till I crumbled in my grief.

Rohanne K Udall (14)
Walthamstow School for Girls, London

The Sick Rose

It all began when I first saw you,
Although we had ups and downs
I knew there was a good turn out to be seen
As our love progressed
I became more attached to you.
I sit here looking at the rose you first got me
The memories flood back to me
I've always kept this rose as a symbol of our love
As the rose fades away slowly
Delicate and precious the way we used to be
It seems like you've faded away from me too.
The rose still has a touch of redness and life
The way my heart still has love for you.

Mariam Malik (14)
Walthamstow School for Girls, London

Pride!

Her gaze burned my back
As I walked away.
What was once a good friend
Had betrayed my trust and feelings.
Tears stung my eyes but I held it all in,
I was not going to let her win.
I slowly moved over to her,
Hearing hear taunts and jeers,
I lashed out.
As she walked away, I felt pride . . .
In her black eye!

Emily Hoeg-Mikkelsen (13)
Walthamstow School for Girls, London

Penguins

Slipping and sliding, occasionally colliding,
On ice can be found tobogganing and gliding,
Emperors, Rockhoppers, Adelies and Kings,
With exquisite black, white and yellow beaks, claws and wings,
Like torpedoes they plunge deep down in the sea,
Away from huge leopard seals, hurriedly they flee,
Huddled together the young penguin chicks stand,
Scattered like pebbles all across the frozen land,
Antarctica is the place where these cool guys chill out,
At their dinner parties they never feed on fresh water trout,
In their tuxedoes they only dine on the finest sea-salted cuisine,
Always keeping their feathers immaculately groomed, neat and
pristine,
Comically they waddle, caricature enhanced,
These peculiar looking creatures make you entranced!

Katie Doherty (14)
Walthamstow School for Girls, London

From The Black Of The Shadows To A World Of Light

As the sun rises the shadows of people
Appear in lots of different positions
Like a swarm of shadows drifting away
In different directions.
It feels like you're in a world of no light,
Only darkness surrounds you,
And the sky has had no appointment from the sun
For when it will bring light into the shadows and darkness.
For once, when the sun and moon will bring light to the world
Below it, only then will be announced
That there is such a thing as light.

Mariam Mir (12)
Walthamstow School for Girls, London

Friends

The road to a friend is never long.
When you feel sad, friends make you strong
Friendship should grow as time goes by,
As you depend on friends when you laugh or cry.
Collecting memories along the way
Loving them more and more each and every day
True friends are few and far between, something precious and close
And when you're feeling down and sad, friends give you hope
Friends don't gossip and tear you down
If you are in need they will be around
Giving freely their time and lending an ear
Talking and encouraging and sharing all your fears
A valued friend is one you can trust and depend
Will keep all your secrets to the very end.

Selina Robinson (15)
Walthamstow School for Girls, London

The Morning Tree And The Night Flower

I wish upon the morning tree,
The flower, the bird and the sea,
That the morning tree will always be.
It will stand strong and tall,
It will never rattle . . .
And may it keep growing conkers so I can battle!

I wish upon the night flower,
The moon, the stars and the darkest hour,
That the night flower will never collapse during any rain shower.
It will always stand strong,
It will never be kicked . . .
And may it always bring friends to be freshly picked!

Demi Slater (11)
Walthamstow School for Girls, London